The Early Detection of Reading Difficulties

Marie M.Clay

Heinemann

Heinemann Publishers
Cnr College Road and Kilham Avenue, Auckland 9,
New Zealand.
The Windmill Press, Kingswood, Tadworth, Surrey KT20
6TG, England.
70 Court Street, Portsmouth, New Hampshire 03801, U.S.A.

Also at Edinburgh, Melbourne, Johannesburg, Ibadan,
Nairobi, Lusaka, New Delhi, Hong Kong, Singapore,
Kuala Lumpur, Kingston, Port of Spain

ISBN 0 86863 276 7
SBN 435 802 410

©1979 Marie M. Clay
First Published 1972
Reprinted 1975, 1976, 1977, 1979
Second edition 1979
Reprinted 1981, 1982, 1983 with corrections
Third edition 1985

The pronouns she and he have often been used in this text to
refer to the teacher and child respectively. Despite a possible
charge of sexist bias it makes for clearer, easier reading if
such references are consistent.

Printed in Hong Kong

Other books by Marie Clay

Reading: The Patterning of Complex Behaviour
Sand (Concepts About Print Test)
Stones (Concepts About Print Test)
What Did I Write?
Reading Begins at Home (Co-author)
Observing Young Readers
Record of Oral Language and Biks and Gutches (Co-author)

The Early Detection of Reading Difficulties

Contents

Introduction

Systematic Observation

I have tried to observe individual children at work reading and writing, and to capture evidence of the progress they make. Science is based on systematic observation of phenomena under known conditions. Physicists or chemists in laboratories, botanists and zoologists in the field, behavioural scientists in psychology, sociology, linguistics, and cultural anthropology all use observation to get research data. Despite some lingering mistrust of observation in educational research it is becoming more acceptable to use direct observation as a method for data collection particularly in the years of early childhood education (Genishi, 1982).

Educators have relied on systematic testing rather than systematic observation of learning. An undue focus on testing can deprive teachers and administrators of valuable information about learners and their learning. There is a seductive efficiency about final assessment scores. Yet a funny thing happens on the way to those final assessments: day to day learning takes place. I am certain that, in education, evaluation needs to pay more attention to the systematic observation of learners who are on the way to those final assessments.

Observing individual progress

Early childhood education has used observations of what children can do because little children often cannot put into words what they are doing or thinking. In the past 25 years studies of how children learn to speak have been exciting. In the 1960s researchers went into homes to observe children learning language and record its use as it occurred in natural settings. They followed the progress of particular children as they developed and their language changed. They studied what actually occurred making precise records, and they did not depend on tests or on recollections of what occurred.

Interest shifted from an early focus on the structures of the language to meaning. In the 1970s this led us to study the effects of the contexts in which language occurs. The young child's language is so related to the things he is talking about that you can have trouble understanding him unless you also know about the things he refers to. We became more sensitive to the ways in which we change our language according to the place we are in, and who we are talking to. We learned more about the ways in which the languages of the homes differ, more about dialects and more about the complexities of bilingual learning.

Attention moved to the detailed study of interactions between mothers and children, teachers and children, children and children. As a result of all this recording of naturally occurring behaviour we now know a great deal about the ways in which the contexts of language interactions facilitate or constrain the development of language in children. We know that entry into formal education settings like schools, reduces children's opportunities for talking, and that some types of programmes prevent children from using the excellent and efficient ways of learning language which they have used before they came to school.

There have been many exciting observational studies of children's writing in the last decade. The young child has emerged as an active participant in the process of becoming a writer. To take only one illustration, the studies of Mexican and Argentinian children by Ferreiro and Teberosky (1982) described the fascinating shifts occurring well before children begin to use the alphabetic principle of letter-sound relationships, which we commonly think if as the beginning of writing. These preschool children were making discoveries about writing, constructing the writing system and making it their own. The observation of writing behaviours has taken us forward in great leaps since 1975.

Observing reading behaviour

The observations of reading behaviours which are described in this book are controlled, and not casual. The child is presented with a text and the teacher records exactly what he says and does. Perfect performance is easy to record. When the performance is less than perfect there are opportunities to record the work done by the child to get it right, to puzzle it out. This reveals something of the processes by which the child monitors and corrects his own performance. When he encounters something new we can observe how he approaches the novel thing, and what he learns from the encounter.

One thing readers do is that they correct some errors without any prompting. Observing this we must ask 'How can this be? Why does the child do that?' One might reply, 'It's something in his memory.' But when one asks what cues the child might have been using one finds consistencies. The child uses cues from the structure of the sentence, or the meaning of the message, or the visual cues of the letters or letter order. We can infer from the kinds of errors and self-corrections that children make, together with their comments, much of what they are attending to.

The learning work which goes on at these moments of choosing between possible responses, is captured in a running record.

Running records of text reading can be used whenever oral reading is appropriate. Teachers can use them in many ways.

1   Capturing behaviour for later consideration. When teachers take a running record as the child reads his book they find they notice more about what the child is trying to do. They can also look back over this record, replay in their minds exactly what the children said and did, check on the validity of their assumptions, and think about the behaviour. The record puts the behaviour of the moment on record.

2   Quantifying the record. If you know how many words the child reads you can quickly turn this behaviour into an accuracy score, and relate this to your gradient of book difficulty. He reads Book Level Seven with 95% accuracy but Book Level Eight with 87% accuracy.

3   A cumulative record. Change over time can be captured with such records taken from time to time, during the child's usual reading to the teacher.

4   Placement. From such records teachers can place children in groups or classes in a school. A child who is changing his school can be quickly checked to see at what level he will succeed in a new school.

5   For critical decisions. Critical decisions about giving the young child special assistance of some kind, or rapid promotion, or a referral to the school psychologist can be supported with a report on the child's reading behaviour on texts, from a running record. I advise my child psychologist students to ask for such records (partly because it puts a responsibility on teachers to be observant and partly because it saves the psychologist's time).

6   To establish text difficulty. I think of reading progress as being able to read increasingly difficult texts with accuracy and understanding. Running records are used by teachers to try out a child on a book to test the difficulty level of the text in relation to the child's competencies. Having such a behavioural record of exactly how a pupil reads a particular text gives teachers confidence to allow different children to move through different books at different speeds. They know they can still keep track of individual progress.

7   Observing particular difficulties. Running records provide opportunities for observing children's confusions and difficulties. The teacher records every correct response with a tick and records all error and self-correction behaviour. This provides evidence of how the child works on words in text, what success he has, and what strengths he brings to the task. A teacher can quickly decide what might be the next most profitable learning point for that child and can test this out during teaching.

8   For research or research purposes. The records of well-trained teachers taken on a series of texts with a known gradient of difficulty can yield a ranking of students on level by accuracy which will correlate highly with test scores in the first two to three years of schooling.

Information for the education system

There are several ways that an education system or a school system or a cluster of classes in a school can gain information on performance in that *system* by observing reading behaviours.

1   Programme emphases. If a supervising teacher takes records of text reading with a wide sample of children she will quickly discover if the teaching programme is out of balance. Word by word reading, spelling out words, not attending to meaning, ignoring the first letter cues or word endings — all these will stand out clearly in the records. And so will the good outcomes like getting it all together smoothly, working on words in ways which surprise the teacher, enjoying the stories and commenting on possible plot and character outcomes, relating what is being read to other experiences.

2   New programme features. If a programme is changed and new emphases are introduced, running records can be used to monitor the effects. Do the desired changes in children's processing of texts show up on the records? Do the records suggest any minor adjustments, now, without waiting for the summative assessment at the end of the year?

3   Training teachers. A running record is an assessment which leads the teacher to ask herself questions about the child's needs. As she takes a record a teacher may discover new behaviours and begin to think about learning in new ways. For example, sometimes the reader goes back, repeating himself, rerunning the correct message. Why does he do that? He was correct. Could this be that the child is surprised by what he read and has rerun to *monitor* his own behaviour to ensure that it is correct? Monitoring one's own language activities has a great deal of relevance for learning. It is important and needs to be encouraged.

Another contribution to teacher training occurs when teachers keep today's record as a baseline, and over several occasions observe the child again, capturing progress. It is informative to look back at the records of the changes that have occurred.

4   Information for lay persons. Two groups who make demands on teachers in New Zealand are parents and administrators. We have been surprised at how impressed both groups have been with two outcomes of running records taken over time. Teachers have used graphs of the reading progress of children through their reading books in their appeals for resources to School Committees and School Boards. Parents have also been reassured by such records and by sharing with the teacher the folios of work which show the child's progressions in writing. We have found that behavioural records, if thoughtfully planned, communicate clearly to lay persons interested in education. Note that it is not the actual running records that have been shared with lay people.

As well as Running Records other observation procedures reported in this early intervention survey are Concepts About Print, Writing Vocabulary, Dictation for Hearing Sounds in Words, and Letter Identification. These can show teachers which children do not understand some basic concepts about books and print, or who is trying to read with little knowledge of letters, or which children seem to know words but are not noticing letter sequences within them. The confusions of young readers belong to all beginners: it is just that the successful children sort themselves out and the unsuccessful do not.

Observation and assessment

It is difficult to design a good reading assessment instrument to use close to the onset of instruction. Standardised tests sample from all behaviours and they do not discriminate well until considerable progress has been made by many of the children (Clay, 1979). Yet teachers can identify their slow progress children before standardised tests can do this. In my own research 20-25% of beginning readers were showing some confusions and difficulties one year to eighteen months before good assessments could be obtained by standardised tests of reading for children in the tail end of the distribution of test scores. It seems as though we should try to use systematic observation by teachers as one way to achieve early identification.

To become observers of the reading process teachers will have to give up looking for a single, short assessment test for the acquisition stages of reading. Children move into reading by different tracks and early assessments must be wide-ranging. If there is a single task that stands up better than any other it is the running record of text reading. This is a neutral observation task, capable of use in any system of reading, and recording progress on whatever gradient of text difficulty has been adopted by the education system.

I have come to place less emphasis on assessments which yield an age or grade level score for the Junior School. By the time one has allowed for the standard error of the score one knows very little about the individual child's needs in learning. A programme of assessment will give me checkpoints on the general level of performance of children but I would want to have, in addition, records of progress on individual children — where they were at various points during the year, what products they could produce and what processes they could control on what texts.

To be acceptable as evidence of children's progress observational data would have to be as reliable as test data. Running records have shown high reliability, with accuracy and error reliabilities of 0.90. Observers find self-correction behaviour harder to agree upon and the reliability can drop to 0.70.

Running records of text reading have face and content validity. You cannot get closer to the valid measure of oral reading than to be able to say the child can read the book you want him to be reading at this or that level with this or that kind of processing behaviour. Little or nothing is inferred. You can count the number of correct words to get an accuracy score. The record does not give a measure of comprehension but you can tell from studying the error and self-correction behaviour whether the child works for meaning. You do not get a score on letters known, but you can see whether the child uses letter knowledge on the run in his reading.

In summary, despite training in measurement, and experience in clinical child psychology I have come to regard normative, standardised tests as having their place, but as indirect ways of observing, suitable for reporting behaviours of groups. By comparison with the observations of learners at work, test scores are approximations or estimates, at times misrepresenting individual progress, and at times presenting results stripped of the very information that is required for designing sound instruction.

To minimise carelessness, bias and variability in observation records:

- there has to be a gradient of difficulty in the texts used for reading.
- the teachers must be well-trained. Six teachers scoring the same record should all get the same results. One teacher reading another teacher's record should be able to replay what the child actually said.

Reading Recovery Procedures . . .

Early identification of children at risk in reading has proved to be possible and should be systematically carried out not later than one year after the child has entered a formal programme. This gives the shy and slow children time to settle in and adjust to the demands of a teacher. It also overcomes the problems of trying to identify those who fail to learn to read before some of them have had a chance to learn what reading is about. In many ways it is sensible to try to predict this only after all children have had some equivalent opportunities to respond to good teaching.

Each child will differ from the other in what is confusing, what gaps there are in knowledge, in ways of operating on print. The failing child might respond to an intervention programme especially tailored to his needs in one-to-one instruction. Teachers who had found the observation procedures useful for identifying the children who were in need of individual help asked me for further guidance. How should they teach those failing children? They were asking for specific teaching procedures which they felt they were not able to invent.

Most of the assumptions about reading achievement and reading difficulty would not lead us to expect that children who have difficulty would ever catch up to their classmates, or make continued *normal* progress. They would have to learn at greatly accelerated rates of progress to do that. The Reading Recovery development programme questioned whether such assumptions were well-founded. We asked how many children given a quality intervention *early* in their schooling could achieve and maintain normal levels of progress? In other words for what percentage of the children having reading difficulties was it really a question of never having got started with appropriate learning patterns?

So the Reading Recovery section of this book is written for those who want to ensure that every child early in schooling moves out from non-reading status and begins to engage with the task of reading books and writing stories.

A quality model of Reading Recovery provides several dimensions of assistance for a child in addition to his class programme.

• Firstly, a shift to one-to-one instruction allows the teacher to design a programme that begins where the child is, and not where the curriculum is. Any grouping of children for teaching forces a compromise on this position.
• Then, daily instruction increases the power of the intervention.
• The teacher strives to make the child independent of her (to overcome one of the major problems of remedial tuition) and she never does for the child anything that she can teach him to do for himself.
• Acceleration is achieved by all the above means and also because the teacher never wastes valuable learning time on teaching something the child does not need to learn. She moves him to a harder text as soon as this is feasible but backs such progressions with quantities of easy reading.

• From sound theory of the reading process the child is taught 'how to . . .', how to carry out operations to solve problems in text, how to monitor his reading, how to check his options, how to be an independent processor of print.

. . .as an Intervention in an Education System

It is not enough to have systematic observation procedures which monitor the progress of individual children. To be really effective a powerful second chance programme must be provided. It must be viable within the education system and it must have its own checks and balances to give quality assurance and quality control. It must 'live' in and adapt to small and large schools, to small and large education systems, and to different populations and reading programmes.

Many interventions for children with special needs never get to consider these issues. It is necessary to demonstrate:

• that the programme can work with children,
• that teachers can be trained to make it work,
• that the programme can fit into the organisation of the schools, and
• that it can be run and maintained within an education system.

In considering those issues I have learned that quality control of an intervention to recover failing children requires:

• that teachers be trained concurrently in the conceptual and practical aspects of the programme,
• that they understand the procedures,
• that they apply them consistently and critically,
• that they can articulate their assumptions and discuss these,
• that they are supervised for a probationary period,
• that their trainers thoroughly understand the theory on which the programme and procedures were based,
• that the teacher is a member of a school team which is mounting the intervention to reduce reading difficulties in that school,
• that the education system support the principles on which an early intervention programme works, supplying resources early to save higher outlay on older children.

For whom is the book written? It is for teachers who want to be careful observers of children learning to read. For those who like to watch children in an open, relatively unsequenced programme of learning to read from story books, the observation procedures will provide a means of monitoring progress. The book is also for teachers who are free to work individually with one or more children having difficulties with reading although we have rarely seen satisfactory programmes devised by teachers who have not been trained in the procedures and in how to mount the programme. (See p.52) It is for administrators who want to read a simple account of what has been achieved in the research projects (p.84) and who wish to achieve the quality control that is necessary to drastically reduce reading difficulties in an education system. One assumes that training will accompany any attempts to use the procedures. Trying to make them work from the written account in this book is unlikely to bring the success that can be achieved in a fully-fledged training programme which includes observation and discussion sessions. (Clay, 1982.)

PART ONE

SYSTEMATIC OBSERVATION

Also - not no time given to sustained (silent) practicing reading or reading for enjoyment. This should be made an integral part of the Nature - at least once per week.

Relate to lectures

Sensitive and systematic observation of young children's reading and writing behaviours provides teachers with feedback which can shape their next teaching moves. Teaching then can be likened to a conversation in which you listen to the speaker carefully before you reply.

the low progress reader

1 The Reading Process

Reading, like thinking, is a complex process. When you think all you have to do is to produce the responses from within you. When you read you have to produce responses which are precisely the ones the author wrote. You have to match your thinking to the author's.

You will be familiar with the old game 'Twenty Questions'. Reading is something like that game. The smarter readers ask themselves the most effective questions for reducing uncertainty; the poorer readers try lots of trivial questions and waste their opportunities to reduce their uncertainty. They do not put the information-seeking processes into effective sequences.

Many remedial programmes direct their students to the trivial questions. All readers, from five year old beginners on their first books to the effective adult reader need to use:

- the meaning
- the sentence structure
- order cues
- size cues
- special features
- special knowledge
- first and last letter cues

before they resort to left to right sounding out of chunks or letter clusters or, in the last resort, single letters. Such an analysis makes the terms 'look and say' or 'sight words' or 'phonics' nonsense as explanations of what we need to know or do in order to be able to read.

Reading for meaning involves the monitoring of cues from all these sources. The high progress reader after one year of instruction, operates on print in an integrated way in search of meaning, and reads with high accuracy and high self-correction rates. He reads with attention focussed on meaning. What he thinks the text will say can be checked by looking for sound-to-letter associations. He also has several ways of functioning according to the difficulty level of the material. Where he cannot grasp the meaning with higher level strategies he can engage a lower gear and use another strategy such as knowledge of letter clusters or letter-sound associations, but manages to maintain a focus on the messages of the text.

On the other hand, the low progress reader or reader at risk tends to operate on a narrow range of strategies. He may rely on what he can invent from his memory for the text but pay no attention at all to visual details. He may disregard obvious discrepancies between his response and the words on the page. He may be looking so hard for words he knows and guessing words from first letters that he forgets what the message is about. Unbalanced ways of operating on print can become habituated and automatic when they are practised day after day. They are very resistant to change and this can happen as early as the first 12 to 18 months of instruction.

That is why a Diagnostic Survey after one year of instruction is so important. Intervention at this stage can help the children who are stumbling to operate on print more appropriately, so they can learn to work effectively under normal classroom conditions and make progress at average rates.

In recent years there have been shifts in our understanding of some psychological processes and yet old theories remain encapsulated in our teaching methods and assumptions. Some of these concepts need to be reviewed here.

By far the most important challenge for the teacher of reading is to change the ways in which the child operates on print to get the messages. We must look briefly at the model of the reading process that is implied here. (A more extensive discussion related to the early years of reading acquisition is available in *Reading: The Patterning of Complex Behaviour*, 1979.)

Reading involves messages expressed in language. Usually it is a special kind of language which is found in books. Children bring to the reading situation a control of oral language but the oral language dialect differs in important ways from the written language dialect. Although some children may not speak a standard oral dialect almost all have a well-developed language system even though they use it differently from speakers of the standard dialect. They have control of most of the sounds of the language, a large vocabulary of words which are labels for quite complex sets of meanings, and they have strategies for constructing sentences.

Reading also involves knowing about the direction rules of printed language, space formats, and punctuation cues — things which the skilled reader is not aware of because he responds automatically to such conventions of print.

Reading involves visual patterns — clusters of words/syllables/blends/letters — depending on how one wants to break the patterns up. The reading process is so automatic in skilled readers that it is only by drastically altering the reading situation that we can show how adults scan text to pick up cues from patterns and clusters of these components. Children tend to operate on visual patterns in very personal ways.

The flow of oral language does not always make the breaks between words clear and young children have some difficulty breaking messages up into words. They have even greater difficulty breaking up a word into its sequence of sounds and hearing the sounds in sequence. This is not strange. Some of us have the same problem with the note sequences in a complicated melody.

These are four different areas of learning which facilitate reading. Language was put first because the meanings embodied in print are of high utility, especially if one already knows something about the topic of the text. Language has two powerful bases for prediction in reading. The first is the meanings and the second is the sentence structures. A third, less reliable and sometimes confusing and distorting source of cues, exists in the letter-sound relationships. Theoretical analyses tell us that it is the consistencies in the spelling patterns or clusters of letters, rather than the letter-sound relationships that assist our reading. If that is where the consistencies lie that is where the human brain will find and use them, even if it has to overcome some of the things that teachers have taught. The conventions that are used to print language need to be learned. They are sometimes the source of some fundamental confusions.

Visual cues are basic for fluent correct responding and skilled readers tend to use visual knowledge in a purely incidental way, just scanning sufficiently to check on the messages of the text. The beginning reader must discover for himself how to scan and visually analyse print to locate cues and features that distinguish between letters and words.

The sound sequences in words are also used in rapid reading to anticipate a word from a few cues or to check a word one is uncertain about. This requires two kinds of detailed analyses in strict co-ordination; the analysis of the sounds in sequence and the visual analysis in left to right sequence.

Today it is accepted that much of what we thought of as 'given' in intelligence is learned during the process of cognitive development. Experience counts in cognitive functioning.

A second concept, persistent in many educational statements is that 'in some rough and ready way' achievement matches to general measured intelligence. We have known for nearly thirty years that when you look at the children who are over-achieving, for example when a child is reading well and several years above his mental age level, then the supposed match between achievement and intelligence must be questioned.

If we put the last two concepts together, — that some part of the cognitive process is learned or realised through experience and that achievement ages rarely match mental ages, — there is plenty of scope for teaching and learning experience to bring about a change in children's attainments.

The third revision of an older position is in the area of brain functioning. When psychologists wrote about the brain as similar to a telephone exchange, association theories of learning were popular and people were thought of as having better or poorer telephone exchanges, prewired to do poorer or better jobs. Without discarding the idea that people may differ in the brain structures they have to work with, it is now known, that for complex functions the brain must call on circuits which link several quite different parts of the brain and that such circuits only become functional for those persons who learn to do those things. We create many of the necessary links in the brain as we learn to engage in particular activities. If we do not learn we do not have the linked pathways.

2 Reading Programmes

Traditional Approaches

Since I first began to work with children with learning difficulties more than 30 years ago the teaching problems have remained much the same, although the services have increased and improved and the percentage of children needing help may have been reduced. What we do have today is an awareness of reading difficulties among teachers, parents and the community that did not exist in the 1940s when we were trying to create that awareness.

With the growth of community interest there has been a proliferation of naive ideas about what reading is and what reading difficulties are. Incorrect and misleading ideas occur in the media each week. The following are two examples.

- Critics of the schools often assume that people differ in intelligence but they expect all people to reach a *imilar* level in reading. These two expectations are contradictory.
- Completely erroneous statements are made about *words seen in reverse* or *the brain scrambling the signals for the eyes* or *squares looking like triangles*. There is no evidence to support such nonsensical descriptions of how our brains work as we read.

These errors of understanding arise from adults who make superficial or poor observations of their own skills or who disseminate misguided interpretations of new concepts, half-understood.

By the fourth year at school a teacher will have a range of reading ability in her classroom that spreads over five or six years. The less able children will read like children in the first or second year class and her more able children will read like young high school pupils. This describes the expectable normal range of reading achievement for which the class teacher must provide. It comes about in part because once a certain command of reading is attained one's reading improves every time one reads. Traditionally a child has been considered worthy of special help only if his achievement falls more than two years below the average for his class or age group. That criterion had more to do with the reliability of our achievement test instruments than to any particular learning needs of the children.

Teachers and the educational system should make every effort to reduce the number of children falling below their class level in reading, but public opinion must learn to ask different evaluative questions. If all children at every point in the range of normal variation are increasing their skill then the school is doing its job well. All children will not be able to read in the same way any more than they can all think alike.

Let me give an example. Livia had many differences in his preschool experiences compared with the average school entrant. He was over seven years before he was able to start reading books. In his fourth year at school he was reading well at a lower Standard One or third year level. In one sense he was not a reading problem. His rate of progress *once he had begun to read* was about average. Livia needed reading material and instruction *at his level* so that he could continue to learn to read and only in that sense had he a reading problem. If put on to fifth year materials he would work at frustration level and could even 'go backwards' because he would no longer be practising, in smooth combination, the skills he had developed so far. In this way he could become illiterate for want of appropriate pacing of his reading material.

There is a reading level below which the child may lose his skill when he moves out into the community rather than maintain it. It falls somewhere around the average 10 to 11 year old reading achievement level. If our reading skill is not sufficient for us to practise it every day by reading the paper or notices, or instructions, then we seem to lose some of the skill in much the same way as we lose a foreign language we no longer speak.

A first requirement of a good reading programme is that all teachers check the provisions that they make for the lowest reading groups in their classes. Is the programme really catering for the range of reading achievement that was recorded on the survey tests of class reading? (In New Zealand these would be tests like the Progressive Achievement Tests of Reading Comprehension and Vocabulary, NZCER, 1969.) It is *very* important to ensure that the difficulty level of the reading material is appropriate. If children in a low reading group are not reading for meaning, if what they read does not sound like meaningful language, if they are stuttering over sounds or words with no basis for prediction, they should be taken back to a level of reading material that they can read accurately, with only one error in five to 10 words. Each classroom needs a wide range of reading books to cater for the expected range of reading skills. Just as you might find it relaxing on holiday to pick up a light novel, an Agatha Christie or a science fiction book, children enjoy easy reading too. *On easy material they practise the skills they have and build up fluency.*

Perhaps one or two children in the lowest group do not seem to be able to read anything. It may be that they have been forced to read at frustration level for as long as a year or two, and that they *have lost their initial reading skills*. Children can go backwards later in their schooling, reading worse than they did at seven years. Such children may need individual teaching in order to re-develop an independent attack on books.

In the lowest reading group of many classes there could be a child who has never started to learn to read. Such children are given remedial attention two and three times a week for two to three years at least and if they are older pupils even this will not make up for those years of lost learning and their associated sense of failure.

What are the ingredients of a good reading programme for children of low achievement in classroom settings? For a good programme you need a very experienced teacher who has been trained to think incisively about the reading process and who is sensitive to individual differences.

You need an organisation of time and place that permits such teachers to work individually with the children who have the least skills. The teacher helps and supports the pupil in reading meaningful messages in texts which are expertly sequenced to the individual's needs.

The teacher aims to produce in the pupil a set of behaviours which will ensure a self-improving system. With a self-improving set of behaviours the more the reader reads the better he gets, and the more unnecessary the teacher becomes.

The teacher expects to end up with pupils who are as widely distributed in reading as they are in the population in intelligence, mathematical achievement, sporting skills or in cooking prowess. But each pupil should be making progress, from where he is to somewhere else.

Frequently, someone approaches me with this kind of statement — 'I'm not a teacher, but I would like to help children with reading difficulties. Do you think I could?' My answer is that the best person to help a child with reading difficulties is a trained teacher, who has become a master teacher of reading, and who has been trained as a specialist in reading problems. There is no room for an amateur approach to children with reading difficulties.

And unlike many human conditions failure to read does not end in spontaneous recovery.

Early Intervention

All understandings of how we read and of what the reading process is, have changed in the last two decades under the impact of reports from intensive research efforts. What the older scholars recommended as techniques still have validity; the ways in which they understood the reading process do not. Theorists now look upon the reading process in a different way and that makes many of the

older books on reading out of date. It is not enough today to recommend old concepts and cures to solve reading difficulties. We now have very good reasons for discarding old concepts that lead to ineffective teaching.

If I believed for example that visual images of words had to be implanted by repetition in children's minds, and that a child had to know every set of letter-sound relationships that occur in English words then I could not explain my successes. I could not explain how an 11-year-old with a reading age of eight years could make three years progress in reading in six months, having two short lessons each week. It just would not be possible. A good theory ought at least to be able to explain its successes.

When I surveyed the many studies which measured children before remedial work, after the programmes, and then after a follow-up period, the results were almost always the same. Progress was made while the teacher taught, but little progress occurred once the clinical programme finished. There was little progress back in the classroom (Aman and Singh, 1983). One study like this carried out in New Zealand recently had the same result. The children could not continue to progress without the remedial teacher. They were not learning reading in the way that successful readers learn. Successful readers learn a system of behaviours which continues to accumulate skills merely because it operates. (Exceptional reading clinicians do help children to build self-improving strategies but they do not seem to do this frequently enough to influence the research findings.)

We have operated in the past on a concept of remedial tuition that worked but did not work well enough. There have been clinicians, principals, teachers, and willing folk in the community working earnestly and with commitment. Individual children have received help but the size of the problem has not been reduced. Some children were recovered, others were maintained with some improvement and some continued to fail. Why? Lack of early identification has been one reason. In other areas of special education we identify our deaf babies, our blind and cerebral-palsied preschoolers get special help to minimise the consequential aspects of their handicap but in reading teachers have often waited until the child's third or fourth year at school before selecting children for remedial instruction. By then the child's reading level is two years behind that of his peers. The difficulties of the young child might be more easily overcome if he had practised error behaviour less often, had less to unlearn and relearn, and still had reasonable confidence in his own ability. Schools must change their organisation to solving these problems early. It only takes a child with the most supportive teacher three to four months at school to define himself as 'no good at that' when the timetable comes around to reading activities.

Teachers and parents of 11- to 16-year-olds often believe that schools have done nothing for the reading difficulties of the young people they are concerned about. Yet the older child has probably been the focus of a whole sequence of well-intentioned efforts to help, each of which has done little for the child. This does not mean that we do not sometimes succeed with a brilliant teacher, a fantastic teacher-child relationship, a hard-working parent-child team. What it does mean is that the efforts often fail *for want of experienced teaching, and for want of persistence and continuity of efforts.* They often fail because they are begun too late.

It seemed to me that the longer we left the child failing the harder the problem became and three years was too long. The results of waiting are these.

• There is a great gap or deficit to be made up.
• There are consequential deficits in other aspects of education.
• There are consequences for the child's personality and confidence.
• An even greater problem is that the child has not failed to learn in his three years at school, he has tried to do his work, he has practised his primitive skills and he has habituated, daily, the wrong responses. He has learned; and all that learning stands like a block wall between the remedial teacher and the responses that she is trying to get established. A remedial programme must take what has to be unlearned into account.

Why have we tended to wait until the child was eight or more years old?
• We believed, erroneously, that children mature into reading.
• We do not like to pressure children, and we gave them time to settle.
• We knew children who were 'late bloomers', (or we thought we did).
• Our tests were not reliable until our programmes were well underway and we were loathe to label children wrongly or to use scarce remedial resources on children who would recover spontaneously.
• We did not understand the reading process sufficiently well.
• We thought a change of method, a search for the great solution, would one day make the reading problem disappear.
• We believed in simple, single causes such as 'not having learned his phonics.'
• Teachers have real difficulty in observing which children are having difficulty at the end of the first year of instruction often claiming there are no such children in their schools.

In 1962 when I began my research I asked the simple question 'Can we see the reading process going wrong in the first year of instruction?' It was, in terms of our techniques at the time an absurd question. The answer is however, that today this can be done by the well-trained teacher. And it is much simpler than administering batteries of psychological tests or trying to interpret the implications for reading of neurological examinations.

At the end of the first year at school, teachers can locate children who can be seen to need extra resources and extra help to unlearn unwanted behaviours or to put together isolated behaviours into a workable system. Simple tests will predict well which young children who have been in instruction for one year, are readers 'at risk'. The test results give the teacher some idea of what to teach next. The second year at school can then be used as a reading recovery year.

The procedures described later in this book were developed in a research programme which focussed on the discovery of what strategies good teachers used with slow readers. We were trying to discover, describe and test which approaches work with failing readers at this level. For two years we worked in a clinical programme. Then we tried out the procedures in five very different schools, and revised our ideas of what will work in the school setting. We made determined efforts to reduce reading failure in 122 six-year-olds and we followed up groups of these children one and three years later.

The Sensitive Observation of Reading Behaviour

First steps in the prevention of reading difficulties can be taken in any school system by the sensitive appraisal of the individuality of school entrants, and the careful observation at frequent intervals of children's responsiveness to a good school programme. Predictive tests may be available but are prone to error because they try to estimate how well a child will perform in an activity he has not even tried yet. They can be supplemented or replaced by systematic observation and recording of what children are doing as they perform the tasks of the classroom. Observation of children's behaviour is a sound basis for the early evaluation of reading progress. Children may stray off into poor procedures at many points during the first year of instruction.

I refer here to a controlled form of observation which requires systematic, objective recording of exactly what a child does on a particular (sometimes contrived) task. It must be carried out without any accompanying teaching or teacher guidance. This contrasts with teaching, with casual, or subjective observation, or with judgemental conclusions based on remembered events from fleeting observations during the teaching of many children.

Of 100 children studied in one Auckland-based study (Clay, 1966, 1982) there were children making slow progress because of poor language development and whose real problem lay in their inability to form and repeat phrases and sentences. There were many children who wavered for months trying to establish a consistent directional approach to print. There were children who could not hear the separation of words within a spoken sentence, nor the sequence of sounds that occur in words. Some children attended only to the final sounds in words. Two left-handed writers had some persisting problems with direction, but so did several right-handed children. For some children with poor motor coordination the matching of words and spaces with speech was a very difficult task. But other children with fast speech and mature language could not achieve success either, because they could not slow down their speech to their hand speed. They needed help with coordinating their visual perception of print and their fast speech. There were unhappy children who were reticent about speaking or writing, and there were rebellious and baulky children. There were children of low intelligence who made slow progress with enthusiasm, and there were others with high intelligence who worked diligently and yet were seldom accurate. There were those who lost heart when promoted because they felt they were not able to cope, and others who lost heart because they were kept behind in a lower reading group.

A flexible programme which respects individuality at first, gradually brings children to the point where group instruction can be provided for those with common learning needs.

While sensitive observation during the first year of instruction is the responsibility of the class teachers, a survey of reading progress after one year of instruction should be programmed by a person responsible for organisation and evaluation within the junior school. Such a survey is held to be desirable and practical, in addition to the activities of class teachers.

A year at school will have given all children a chance to settle, to begin to engage with the reading programme, to try several different approaches, to be forming good or bad habits. It is not hurrying children unduly to take stock of their style of progress a year after society introduces them to formal instruction. Indeed, special programmes must then be made available for those children who have been unable to learn from the standard teaching practices. This makes good psychological and administrative sense.

The timing of such a systematic survey will depend upon the policies of the education system regarding:

- entry to school and
- promotion and/or retention.

In New Zealand continuous entry on children's fifth birthdays is usually followed by fixed annual promotion to the third year class level. This allows a flexible time allocation of 18 to 36 months for the first two class levels according to an individual child's needs. A slow child who takes a year to settle into the strange environment of school may need extra help in the second year to make average progress before promotion to level or class three.

A different scenario would occur with fixed age of entry. Children entering school at one time (four-and-a-half to five-and-a-half, or five-and-a-half to six-and-a-half) would be surveyed within or after their first year at school. My preference would be for them to receive individual help at the beginning of the second year having been promoted rather than retained. An alternative would be to get help to them after six months of the first year on the assumption that they could be promoted to the second year class rather than retained. This latter procedure may have some unforeseen problems in it as it may identify for help children who would 'take off' without help in the second six months of that first year of school.

In school systems where entry occurs at younger ages more relaxed and less urgent policies can be adopted and the end of the first year of schooling seems a suitable time for early identification. In systems where entry age levels tend to be higher, formal instruction tends to proceed with more urgency and waiting for a year before identifying children may not be seen as appropriate. The key point to bear in mind is that children must not be left practising inappropriate procedures for too long, but on the other hand they cannot be pressured and hurried into learning the fundamental complexities of reading and writing. This leads us back to the child who is having difficulty with school learning towards the end of his first year at school. Each child having difficulty will have different things he can and cannot do. Each will differ from the other in what is confusing, what gaps there are in knowledge, in ways of operating on print. The failing child might respond to an intervention programme especially tailored to his needs in one-to-one instruction.

The Early Detection of Reading Difficulties

Traditionally reading difficulties have been assessed with readiness tests, intelligence tests, and tests of related skills such as language abilities or visual discrimination. These have been used to predict areas which might account for a child's reading failure. The problem with the intricate profiles that such tests produce is that while they may sketch some strengths and weaknesses in the child's behaviour repertoire, they do not provide much guide as to what the teacher should try to teach the child *about reading*. The child with limited language skills must still be taught to read, although some authorities advise teachers to wait until the child can speak well. The child with visual perception difficulties can be put on a programme of drawing shapes and finding paths through mazes and puzzles, but he must still be taught to read.

Many research studies have found no benefit resulting from training programmes derived directly from such test results. The pictorial and geometric stimuli used with young retarded readers did not produce gains in reading skill. And oral language training was no more useful. This may well be because the children were learning to analyse data which they did not require in the reading task and they were not learning anything that was directly applicable in the reading activity. Again and again research points to the egocentric, rigid and inflexible viewpoint of the younger, slower or retarded reader. And yet statements on remediation just as often recommend training the child on 'simpler' materials — pictures, shapes, letters, sounds — all of which require a large amount of skill to transfer them to the total situation of reading a message which is expressed in sentence form! To try to train children to read on pictures and shapes or even on puzzles, seems a devious route to reading. One would not deny that many children need a wide range of supplementary activities to compensate for barren preschool lives; but it is foolish to prepare for reading by painting with large brushes, doing jig-saw puzzles, arranging large building blocks, or writing numbers. Preparation for reading can be done more directly with written language.

Having established that printed forms are the remedial media, one can then allow that simplification, right down to the parts of the letters, may at times be required for some children. However, *the larger the chunks of printed language the child can work with, the quicker he learns,* and the richer the network of meanings he can use. We should only dwell on detail long enough for the child to discover its existence and then encourage the use of it in isolation, only when absolutely necessary. As a reader the child will use detail within, and as a part of a pattern of cues or stimuli. The relationships of details to patterns in reading have often been destroyed by our methods of instruction. It is so easy for us as teachers, or for the designers of reading materials, to achieve that destruction.

There have been many attempts to match teaching methods to the strengths of groups of children. The child with good visual perception is said to benefit from sight-word methods; the child with good auditory perception is thought to make better progress on phonic methods. One author writes, 'Children are physiologically oriented to visual or auditory learning'. Another says, 'Teaching phonics as a relatively "pure" form will place a child at a disadvantage if he is delayed in auditory perceptual ability'! Such instruction would place all children at a severe disadvantage; they would have to learn by themselves many skills that their teachers were not teaching, if they were to become successful readers.

Such matching attempts are simplistic, for English is a complex linguistic system. The way to use a child's strengths and improve his weaknesses is not to work on one or the other but to design the tasks so that he practises the weakness with the aid of his strong ability. Rather than take sides on reading methods which deal either with sounds that are synthesised or with sentences which are analysed,

> . . . it is appropriate to select reading texts which are simple and yet retain the full power of semantic and syntactic richness, helping the child to apply his strong abilities to their analysis on any level of language.

Close observation of a child's weaknesses will be needed because he will depend on the teacher to structure the task in simple steps to avoid the accumulation of confusions. For one child the structuring may be in the visual perception area. For another it may be in sentence patterns. For a third it may be in the discrimination of sound sequences. For a fourth it may be in directional learning.

It therefore seems appropriate to seek diagnosis of those aspects of the reading process which are weak in a particular child soon after he has entered instruction. The Diagnostic Survey has been used to provide such information for children taught in very different programmes for beginning reading (in New Zealand, Scotland, Australia and U.S.A.). Children in different instruction programmes do not score in similar ways but the Diagnostic Survey provides a framework within which early reading behaviour can be explored irrespective of the method of instruction. What will vary from programme to programme will be the typical scores on the tests of the Survey after a fixed time in instruction.

In what follows some procedures are outlined that have been found useful for the early detection of reading difficulties. Behind these recommendations lies the belief that it is desirable:

• to observe precisely what children are saying and doing
• to use tasks that are close to the learning tasks of the classroom (rather than standardised tests of reading)

• to observe what children have been able to learn (not what they have been unable to do)
• to discover what reading behaviours they should now be taught from an analysis of performance in reading texts, not from pictorial or puzzle material, or from normative scores
• to shift the child's reading behaviour from less adequate to more adequate responding, by training on reading tasks rather than training visual perception or auditory discrimination as separate activities.

There is only slight emphasis on scores and quantifying progress. The real value of the Diagnostic Survey is to uncover what a particular child controls and what operations and items he could be taught next.

Reading instruction often focusses on items of knowledge, words, letters and sounds. Most children respond to this teaching in active ways. They search for links between the items and they relate new discoveries to old knowledge. They operate on print as Piaget's children operate on problems, searching for relationships which order the complexity of print and therefore simplify it.

The end-point of *early* instruction has been reached when children have a self-improving system, which means that they learn more about reading every time they read, independent of instruction. When they read texts of appropriate difficulty for their present skills, using their knowledge of oral and written language and their knowledge of the world, they use a set of operations or strategies 'in their heads' which are just adequate for reading the more difficult bits of the text. In the process they engage in 'reading work', a deliberate effort to solve new problems with familiar information and procedures. They notice new things about words, and constructively link these things to both their knowledge of the world around them, and to their knowledge of the printed language gained in their short history of successful reading of simple books. The process is progressive and accumulative. The newly-noticed feature(s) of print, worked upon today, becomes the reference point for another encounter in a few days. 'Television' as a new word becomes a reference point for 'telephone' in a subsequent text. Children are working on two theories — what Smith (1978) calls their theory of the world and what will make sense, and a second theory of how written language is created. They are testing these two theories and changing them successively as they read more books.

In the Diagnostic Survey an emphasis will be placed on the operations or strategies that are used in reading, rather than on test scores or on disabilities.

The terms *operation* or *strategy* are used for mental activities initiated by the child to get messages from a text.

A child may have the necessary abilities but may not have learned how to use those abilities in reading. Therefore he will not be observed to use helpful strategies. *He must learn how to...*

Or a child may have made insufficient development in one ability area (say, motor coordination) to acquire the required strategy (say, directional behaviour) without special help. *He must learn how to in spite of...*

Again a child may have items of knowledge about letters and sounds and words but be unable to relate one to the other, to employ one as a cross-check on the other. *He must learn how to check on his own learning...*

In any of these instances the task for the reading recovery programme is to get the child to learn to use any and all of the strategies or operations that are necessary to read texts of a given level of difficulty.

There is an important assumption in this approach. Given a knowledge of some items, and a *strategy* which can be applied to similar items to extract messages, the child then has a general way of approaching new items. We do not need to teach him the total inventory of items. Using the strategies will lead the reader to the assimilation of new items of knowledge. Strategies for thinking about printed language are an important part of a self-improving system.

An example may help to clarify this important concept. Teachers through the years have taught children the relationship of letters and sounds. They have, traditionally, shown letters and given children opportunities to associate sounds with those letters. There seemed to be an obvious need to help the child to translate the letters in his book into the sounds of spoken words. And, in some vague way, this also helped the child in his spelling and story writing.

In our studies of children after one year of instruction we found children at risk in reading who could give the sounds of letters but who found it impossible to hear the sound sequences in the words they spoke. They could go *from letters to sounds* but they were unable to check whether they were right or not because they could not hear the sound sequence in the words they spoke. They were unable to go *from sounds to letters*. Being able to carry out the first operation, letters to sounds, probably leads easily to its inverse for many children but for some of our children at risk one strategy did not imply the other.

After six months of special tutoring Tony's progress report at the age of 6:3 emphasises not the item gains (in Letter Identification or Reading Vocabulary) but the actions or operations that he can initiate. He can analyse some initial sounds in words, uses language cues, has a good locating response, checks his predictions and has a high self-correction rate.

Tony

• (aged 5:9) has some early concepts about directionality and one-to-one correspondence but his low letter identification score and nil scores on word tests mean that he has no visual signposts with which to check his fluent book language.

• (aged 6:0) has made only slight progress in the visual area. In reading patterned text, he relies heavily on language prediction from picture clues and good memory for text, with very little use of visual information. His self-correction behaviour is almost nil, the two corrections made were on the basis of known words.

• (aged 6:3) identifies 37/54 letter symbols, has started accumulating a reading and writing vocabulary and can analyse some initial sounds in words. In reading unpatterned text, he uses language cues, a good locating response, known reading vocabulary and some initial sounds to check his predictions. He has a high self-correction rate.

A reading recovery approach which emphasises the acquisition of reading strategies by-passes questions of reading levels and learning disabilities. It demands the recording of what the child does, on tests of specified difficulty, it refers to the strengths and weaknesses of his strategies, and compares these with a model of the strategies used by children who make satisfactory progress in reading and whose strategies make up a self-improving system.

In a sense it is an economical approach to helping children with reading failure, because it is:

• based on the work of experienced class teachers
• based on early identification
• carried out by class teachers of experience
• directed to strategies or operations which generate further *appropriate* behaviour
• directed towards independence in reading with a self-improving system of reading behaviours as the end goal of the programme.

3 The Diagnostic Survey

The Diagnostic Survey which I have recommended for use with children in their first year of school, and particularly with children at the end of that first year, tries to get away from the concept of tests, and is closer to criterion-referenced assessment. However, the techniques enable teachers to observe children at work on the actual tasks, noting their strengths and their confusions.

A set of standard observation procedures for recording reading and writing behaviours has a number of classroom applications. Various kinds of bias can affect such observations (see p.3) and it is necessary to make our interpretations as reliable as we can. This can be achieved by:

- using standard procedures,
- becoming skilled at applying the procedures,
- using a wide range of observations which can be checked one against the other.

In this Diagnostic Survey several observation techniques are described. *No one technique is satisfactory on its own.* Teachers are advised to apply as many as possible to the children for whom important instructional decisions must be made. Reducing the scope of our observations increases the risk that we will make erroneous interpretations. For example, the Concepts About Print test should not be used in isolation because it assesses only one aspect of early reading behaviours.

Selection of Children

Taking into account the time a child has been at school, select for further study all those who are not obviously making good progress at the end of their first year of instruction. In New Zealand schools this would be on the child's sixth birthday (6:0). This will probably include 30 to 50 percent of the class. The time required for such a survey must be set against the teaching time that is devoted to failing readers further on in the education system. School Principals must become convinced of this preventive need.

There are several reasons why the sixth birthday seems a better checkpoint than the end of the school year in New Zealand schools. This would stagger the testing load throughout the year and would therefore ensure more individual consideration for each child. An end of year survey would be time-consuming and the range of tests applied would tend to be reduced. Class surveys at other times for other reasons will have their own value but

should be additional to a systematic check at the end of the first year of instruction.

To teach yourself something about these procedures it would be a good idea to make an individual case study. Select a child who has been in instruction for one year and who is making some progress but is clearly having difficulties, and try out the procedures.

Although these techniques can be used productively with older failing readers it is important to first gain skill in administration and interpretation of the Diagnostic Survey on the young children for whom it was designed.

A Record of Reading Behaviour on Books

Text difficulty and text type

Throughout schooling reading progress is indicated by satisfactory reading of increasingly difficult texts. New strategies are developed by the reader to cope with increases in the difficulty level of the texts when complexities like multisyllabic words or literary forms of sentence structure are introduced.

When the text is close to natural language the frequently-occurring words of English are read over and over again and the combinations of sounds typically found in English words occur in their natural frequencies. These frequencies are the naturally-occurring equivalents of vocabulary and letter-sound controls imposed in the past on many texts for young readers. Their existence seems to have been overlooked by the advocates of reading texts with controlled vocabulary.

If a child is moving up a practical ladder of difficulty on natural language texts which exercise minimum control over structures and vocabulary, and if he achieves 90% to 95% accuracy by the end of a normal teaching contact with that material he will be getting the opportunity to practise both the words he needs to learn and the clusters of sounds in those words that will help him to analyse new words.

The 'ifs' in the last paragraph imply that we must get reliable measures of how well children read their books because this is important information for planning day to day instruction. Running records, described below, have proved useful in this respect.

The pivotal observation in the Diagnostic Survey, without which all others could be misleading, is a running record of text reading. It is similar to Goodman and

Burke's miscue analysis (1972) but it is more adapted to the teacher's needs in day to day activities of the classroom, particularly for those who teach young children. Running records are taken without marking a prepared script. They may be done on any piece of paper. With practice teachers can take a running record at any time, anywhere, on any text because the opportunity arises or because the behaviour of the moment needs to be captured. Teachers do not need a tape-recorder. They do not have to carry out a long subsequent analysis of the record, and they do not need a technical knowledge of linguistic concepts to derive benefit from the record.

Teachers use running records for instructional purposes to guide their decisions about any of the following:
- the evaluation of text difficulty
- the grouping of children
- the acceleration of a child
- monitoring progress of children
- allowing different children to move through different books at different speeds and yet keeping track of (and records of) individual progress
- observing particular difficulties in particular children.

For critical decisions such as those made in an early detection survey, or decisions about promotion or the provision of special assistance, or to inform a psychologist of the child's progress it would be wise to obtain running records on materials from at least three levels of difficulty:
- an easy text   95-100% correct
- an instructional text 90-94% correct
- a hard text   80-89% correct

The current book (or selection from that book) will usually provide the instructional level.

These three samples provide valuable insights into *strengths* (on the easier materials) and *weaknesses* (on the more difficult materials).

For the classroom teacher it is preferable to use text materials that are part of her everyday programme, and a visitor to the school (such as a reading adviser, a speech therapist or a school psychologist) should ask the class teacher for the book the child is working on at present, and for her suggestions about texts that are *just a little* harder or easier in her programme.

However, if there are reasons why such judgements are not easily made, for example because the class does not use any recognisably graded sets of materials, the teacher or observer may wish to have a standard set of graded paragraphs. From these the observer can select paragraphs which provide evidence of reading skills on three levels of difficulty which reveal strengths, and weaknesses.

Learning to Take a Running Record

Learning to take a running record can unsettle teachers. Those who are used to standardised tests and norms suspect the simplicity of the behaviour records, and so do people who do not like standardised testing.

There is not a lot to learn before you begin record taking, just a few conventions. There is no reason to study a new set of concepts or understand something new about the reading process. The first step is a matter of action. You set yourself the task of recording everything that a child says and does as he tries to read the book you have chosen. Once you begin such recording, and after about two hours of initial practice, no matter how much you might be missing, you have made a good start. The more you take the records the more you will notice about the child's behaviour. It is not a case of knowing everything first and then applying it. Try yourself out and you will begin to notice a few things that you have not noticed before. Practise some more and you will notice more. As your ear becomes tuned-in to reading behaviours and you gain control over the recording conventions your records will become more and more reliable.

I had been teaching reading and remedial reading for many years when I began my research on emergent reading behaviour. I am still humble about the fact that I had really never noticed self-correction behaviour until I started recording everything that children were doing. Then I found that I had been missing something that was very important.

What we are observing and recording is not something that is peculiar to the child who is learning to read. If I take some adult volunteers and ask them to read some ordinary everyday reading materials their reading behaviour can be broken down so that we can observe the same kinds of behaviour that you can observe in children's reading. A smudgy carbon or a bad stencil or a Churchill speech in i.t.a. or a misprint in the newspaper where the lines have been misplaced, such texts will break down the reading behaviours of these competent adults and one can observe self-correction, word-by-word reading and even the use of a pointing finger to locate themselves on the text. Everybody's reading behaviour can be broken down under difficulties.

Make a record of each child reading his three books or book selections. Use ticks for each correct response and record every error in full. A sample reading of 100 to 200 words from each text is required. This should take about 10 minutes. At the early reading level when the child is reading the very simplest texts the number of words may fall below 100 but if three texts are attempted (selected from caption books or first readers or teacher-made books or child-dictated text) this will be satisfactory.

A suggested format for a Running Record Summary Sheet can be found on page 109 and procedures for calculating accuracy and self-correction rates on page 115 of this book.

Some conventions used for recording

1   Mark every word read correctly with a tick (or check). A record of the first five pages of the *Ready to Read* book *Early in the Morning*, that was 100 percent correct would look like this.

Bill is asleep	✓	✓	✓
'Wake up, Bill,' said Peter.	✓ ✓	✓ ✓	✓
Sally is asleep.	✓	✓	✓
'Wake up, Sally,' said Mother.	✓ ✓	✓ ✓	✓
Father is shaving.	✓	✓	✓

2   Record a wrong response with the text under it.

Child:	*home*
Text:	house

3   If a child tries several times to read a word, record all his trials.

Child:	*here*	*h—*	*home*
Text:	house		

Sounding out may be recorded in lower case, n-o-t and spelling the letters in capitals N-O-T.

4   If a child succeeds in correcting a previous error this is recorded as 'self-correction' (written SC).

Child:	*where*	*we*	*when*	SC
Text:	were			

Example **3** does not end in self-correction.

5   If no response is given to a word it is recorded with a dash. Insertion of a word is recorded over a dash.

No response
Child:	—
Text:	house

Insertion
Child:	*here*
Text:	—

6   If the child baulks, unable to proceed because he is aware he had made an error and cannot correct it, or because he cannot attempt the next word, he is told the word (written T).

Child:	*home*	
Text:	house	T

7   An appeal for help (A) from the child is turned back to the child for further effort before using T as in **6** above.

Child:	—	*A*	*here*
Text:	house	—	T

8   Sometimes the child gets into a state of confusion and it is necessary to extricate him. The most detached method of doing this is to say 'Try that again', marking TTA on the record. This would not involve any teaching, but the teacher may indicate where the child should begin again.

It is a good idea to put square brackets around the first set of muddled behaviour, enter the TTA, remember to count that as one error only (see page 20), and then begin a fresh record of the problem text. An example of this recording would be this.

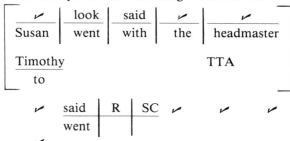

9   Repetition is not counted as error behaviour. Sometimes it is used to confirm a previous attempt. Often it results in self-correction. It is useful to record it as it often indicates how much sorting out the child is doing. 'R' standing for repetition, is used to indicate repetition of a word, with R_2 or R_3 indicating the number of repetitions. If the child goes back over a group of words, or returns to the beginning of the line or sentence in his repetition, the point to which he returns is shown by an arrow.

Child:	*Here is the home*	R	SC
Text:	Here is the house		

10   Directional attack on the printed text is recorded by telling the child to 'Read it with your finger'.

Left to right	L	⟶ R
Right to left	L	⟵ R
Snaking		⇄
Bottom to top	B	⟶ T

For special purposes teachers or researchers may wish to develop their own conventions for scoring other behaviours which they notice. Some behaviours may be specific to, or important for, a particular teaching programme. For example, pausing can be recorded by a slash, /. Some researchers who have been concerned with the length of pausing have used a convention borrowed from linguistics which allows for pauses of four different lengths. These are quickly recorded as

/   //   ⊬   ⧣

I would caution against attention to pausing unless there is a special reason for wishing to record it. *In research studies it has not yet yielded clear messages about the reading process.* It adds little to the teacher's interpretation of her record and may add confusion. *It would be important not to read into a record of pausing interpretations for which there was no other evidence.*
A running record from a child who is making many errors is harder to take and score but the rule is to record all behaviour, and analyse objectively what is recorded.

Reliability
Taped recordings of such reading observations taken from four children over the period of one year were available and were used to check on the reliability of such records (0.98 for error scoring and 0.68 for self-correction scoring, Clay 1966).
A number of trends became obvious during these reliability tests.

• For beginning readers, observers can take running records which give reliable accuracy scores with a small amount of training.
• The effect of poor observation is to reduce the number of errors recorded and increase the accuracy rate. As the observer's skill in recording at speed increases, so the error scores tend to rise.
• To record all error behaviour in full, as against only tallying its occurrence, takes much more practice (but provides more evidence of the child's strategies).
• Observations for poor readers require longer training to reach agreement on scoring standards because of the complex error behaviour.

• Information is lost in the taped observation, especially motor behaviour and visual survey, but observation of vocal behaviour tends to be improved.
• Reliability probably drops as reading accuracy level falls because there is more error behaviour to be recorded in the same time span.
For research work the most reliable records would be obtained by scoring an observation immediately following its manual recording, and re-checking immediately with a taped observation.

Analysing the reading record
From the running record of reading behaviour containing all the child's behaviour on his current book, consider what is happening as the child reads.

Some conventions for scoring the records
In counting the number of errors, some arbitrary decisions must be made but the following have been found workable.

1   Credit the child with any correct or corrected words.

Child:	*to the shops*	Errors: 2
Text:	for the bread	
Score:	✗ ↙ ✗	

2   There is no penalty for trials which are eventually correct.

Child:	*Want*	*won't*	*went*	(SC) Errors: 0
Text:	Went			Self-correction : 1
Score:	—	—	↙	

Child:	*Where*	*we*	*when*	*were*	(SC) Errors: 0
Text:	were				Self-correction: 1
Score:	—	—	—	↙	

3   Insertions add errors so that a child can have more errors than there are words in a line.

Child:	*The train went toot, toot, toot*	Errors: 5
Text:	The little engine sighed	
Score:	↙ ✗ ✗ ✗ ✗ ✗	

4   However, the child cannot receive a minus score for a page. The lowest page score is 0.

5   Omissions. If a line or sentence is omitted each word is counted as an error.

If a page is omitted (perhaps because two pages were turned together) they are not counted as errors. Note that, in this case, the number of words on that page must be deducted from the Running Words Total before calculation.

6   Repeated errors. If the child makes an error (e.g. 'run' for 'ran') and then substitutes this word repeatedly, it counts as an error every time; but substitution of a proper name (e.g. 'Mary' for 'Molly') is counted only the first time.

7   Multiple errors and self-corrections. If a child makes two or more errors (e.g. reads a phrase wrongly) each word is an error. If he then corrects all these errors each corrected word is a self-correction.

8   Broken words. Where a word is pronounced as two words (e.g. a/way) even when this is backed up by pointing as if it were two words, this is regarded as an error of pronunciation not as a reading error unless what is said is matched to a different word. Such things as 'pitcher' for 'picture' and 'gonna' for 'going to' are counted as correct.

9   Inventions defeat the system. When the young child is creatively producing his own version of the story the scoring system finally breaks down and the judgement 'inventing' is recorded for that page, story or book.

10   'Try that again'. When the child is in a tangle this instruction, which does not involve teaching, can be given. It counts as one error and only the second attempt is scored.

11   Fewest errors. If there are alternate ways of scoring responses a general principle is to choose the method that gives the *fewest* possible errors as in B below.

A   *Child:*   *We   went for the bread*
   Text: You went to the shop for the bread
   Score: ×   ✓   ×   ✓   ×   ×   ×   ×
                                         Errors: 6

B   *Child:*   *We   went   for the bread*
   Text: You went to the shop for the bread
   Score: ×   ✓   ×   ×   ×   ✓   ✓   ✓
                                           Errors: 4

Check directional movement

Ask the child to '*Read it with your finger.*'. While this may not be a desirable teaching instruction it is a necessary one for the observer to elicit evidence of directional movement. Record which hand was used, on which page, and the direction of movement.

In a study of children's early learning of directional movement across English texts a common progression was noted (Clay, 1982). There was an early period of confusion as the children tried to orient to the spatial characteristics of the open book. Then there was a period when the child seemed to prefer to use a particular hand for pointing to any text. Finally a more flexible set of behaviour emerged when the child could use either hand on either page without having to pay much attention to direction. As these stages were worked through, sometimes rapidly and sometimes over several months, lapses from directional behaviours were observed. Children might go from right to left or even from bottom to top. Left and right handed children showed similar kinds of behaviours.

Three groups of children have difficulty as beginning readers in disciplining their behaviour within the directional constraints of written language.

• The first group are children who have poor motor coordination or who are inattentive to where their bodies are and how they are arranging their movements.
• The second group are fast-reacting, impulsive children who act before they think and who have great difficulty in governing their responses within any constraints. They can very readily settle into undesirable patterns of responding.
• A third group of beginners at risk are those who do not like to try because they might make a mistake. As the development of directional behaviour involves exploring two-dimensional space, being wrong, and discovering how to behave correctly, children who are too tense, inhibited or timid, may be reluctant to try out a range of directional behaviour. They take longer to learn to discard the poor responses and retain the good ones.

The technique of asking a child to 'Read it with your finger' will only reveal directional behaviour on the gross schema of line scanning. Beyond this there must be some very important visual perception learning to be done. It relates to the scanning of letters and clusters of letters. There are further important orientation behaviours to be learned to do with what the eyes are attending to, in what order, which will not be picked up in observations of pointing behaviour.

Record your observations and comments on directional movement on your summary sheet (pp.109, 111). Any lapse from appropriate directional behaviour is important and should be noted. We are not merely concerned with the child who habitually moves in the wrong direction, but rather with the child who is inconsistent, or in the process of learning directional control shown by lapses from time to time.

Calculate the error rate

Compare the number of errors with the number of running words. Does the child read his book with one error in every five running words of text (which is poor) or is it more like one in twenty (which is good)? Record on the Summary of Running Record Sheet.

Calculate the percentage of errors (see Conversion Table page 115). If there is more than 10 percent of error in the record rate this is a 'hard' text for this child. (For the average child there is movement from 90 percent accuracy when he is first promoted to a book to 95 percent or more as he completes his learning on that book.)

When the child reads a book with less than 90 percent accuracy it is difficult for him to judge for himself whether his attempt at a word is a good one or a poor one. He needs easier material which he can attempt at a rate of not more than one error in ten words at the time he begins the new book. The reading text should use language that comes readily to him. In the very earliest stages it is sometimes necessary to repeat the text until he has almost memorised it, but not quite. Then it will come readily to the tip of his tongue. It is as if the words he needs are stored in the depths of his memory and have to be assisted to float to the surface. The child's own dictated stories provide good reading texts for just this reason — the words and construction of the text should be readily recalled.

If the text is in a different style from that which the child usually reads his error rate will increase because he is predicting from the baseline of old expectations which are inappropriate for the present text.

Error behaviour

To read a continuous text the child must use a variety of skills held in delicate balance. Specific weaknesses or strengths can upset that balance. There are some questions about the errors for a particular child that can guide the teacher's analysis of the behaviour record. (See also Clay, 1979.)

Oral language skills. Are these good enough to make the reading of this text possible? (For instance, could the child repeat the sentences of the text if you asked him to, one by one?) Or, is his language so fluent that the co-ordination of visual perception and motor movement with language is difficult?

Speed of responding. The rate at which a child reads and the time spent on pausing and processing cues are at this level poor indicators of the child's progress. One child may read with the fluency of oral language but may be a poorer reader than another child who pauses and engages in much self-correction behaviour. At this particular stage in reading progress it is good for the child making average progress to be concerned about error and to rectify error if possible. It is poor to maintain fluency and not to notice that one has made an error.

Fast responding can be an indication that language is dominating the reading process allowing for little visual search to take place.

What cues does he depend on?
• Does the child use meaning? If what he reads makes sense, even though it is inaccurate, then he is probably applying his oral language knowledge to his reading.
• Is what he says grammatical? If it is, his oral language is influencing his responding. If it is not, there may be two reasons. Perhaps his language skill is limited and his personal 'grammar' does not contain the structures used in his reading book. Or, if he is paying close attention to detail, or to word by word reading, he may not be allowing his control over English syntax to influence his choices.
• Does he use visual cues from the letters and words?
• Does he read word by word as if recalling each word from a memory bank, unrelated to what has gone before? He may not realise that reading is like speaking, and that his language behaviour is a rich source of help in choosing correct reading responses.

To work out whether the child is responding to the different kinds of cues that could be used you need to *look at every error* that the child makes and ask yourself 'Now what made him say that?' 'Did he miss out on the visual cues?' 'Was he ignoring meaning?'. It is misleading if you do this selectively; you must analyse every error and count those that show this or that kind of cue. You want to be able to conclude, on sound evidence, that 'He pays more attention to visual cues than to meaning', or 'He is guided by structure and meaning but does not search for visual cues'. It is only when you go to the trouble of analysing all the errors that you really get any indication of what his strategies are on reading.

When teachers are familiar with taking running records they may want to write M for meaning, S for structure and V for visual cues on the record form and to record, by circling, which cues the child was using. (See record sheets p. 109). Notice that what you are recording in this case is your best guess: you cannot know what cues the child used. A record may show one, two or three types of cues used on any one error. If you write M S V alongside each error or self-correction and circle the cues you think the child used, the uncircled letters will then show the cues neglected.

Consider the error first. What cues *up to that error* was the child using? Think only of the information the child had before the error occurred. Then consider the self correction. What extra information did the child use in the self correction?

Enter comments on the Analysis of Errors. (Summary of Running Record Sheet.)

Cross-checking strategies

Can the child check one kind of information with another? Can he get movement and language occurring together in a linked or coordinated way? Does he check on language prediction by looking at some letters? Can he hear the sounds in a word and check whether the expected letters are there? A child with outstanding memory for what he hears or with very fast language production often has difficulty in slowing up enough to enable him to learn the visual discriminations. Yet good readers search for cues from different sources which confirm a response. (See pages 72 to 74 and Clay 1979 for further discussion of these reading behaviours.)

Self-correction

Observe and enter in the running record any self-correction behaviour. The child discovers cues that tell him something is wrong. He is aware that a particular message is to be communicated and tries to discover this by using cues. Efficient self-correction behaviour is an important skill in good reading. Calculate the self correction rate (see page 19). A self-correction rate of one in three to five errors is good but one in twenty errors is a very low rate. However the prognosis is good, because self-correction does exist!

Self-correction rates vary greatly. This is because they are not absolute scores: they are always relative measures. They vary with text difficulty, with error rate, with accuracy, and with effort. They cannot be understood unless they are interpreted together with text difficulty and accuracy scores.

If self-correction is evident but inefficient it is a good prognosis. Its absence in a record which contains errors is a danger sign. A child who is making errors and is not aware of this, or who makes no attempt to correct himself, is in difficulties. He is not aware of the need to decode a precise message or he is not aware of the existence of cues, or he does not know how to use them, or he does not try to solve the problem.

If a child engages in a confusion of unsuccessful attempts to solve his errors he needs to learn better bases for making his decisions. His teacher must deliberately teach some priorities like 'Sound the first letter', 'Go back to the beginning of the line', 'What would make sense?' — whichever she judges to be the technique with the highest pay-off in terms of progress, for this child at this time. (See page 73.)

Linda was 5:9 when she was reading the book which gave rise to the example of reading behaviours on the next page. (It was not a very helpful book for her level of reading on the next page.) You might think that she was a poor reader. Yet when you think about what is going on in this record, and how many things she is trying to do, and what kinds of cues she is testing out, you can see that she really is working hard to relate one kind of information to another. This is a very interesting record of her behaviour, showing how active she is in searching, and checking. In time she must become more efficient at doing these things.

An example of very complicated word-solving and self-correction behaviour

Response to I like the swing. I shall get on it. The swing went up and down. It went ...	Interpretation of Behaviour		
	Tries	**Decides**	**Reasons**
I like the swing	Correct		
I shall ke — get	Anticipates wrongly	Corrects	Letter cue?
off it — on it	Anticipates wrongly	Corrects	Meaning?
The swing will — No!	First letter cue	Rejects	Word form?
wa — want	Three letters similar	Rejects	Meaning?
won't (up) — No!	Structure cue 'The swing won't...' plus three letters.	Rejects	Following structure 'won't up'?
will take	New idea	Rejects	One pattern for two responses
we — *wa — No*	A more analytic approach	Rejects	Sounds do not aid recall
(I get mixed up)		'I am confused'	There is always some cue that does not fit
(I'll read it again)	A new approach	Return to the line beginning	'A clean slate'
The swing want	It looks like 'want'	Rejects	Meaning?
*won't up and down	It looks like 'won't'	*Accepts	Fits letter and meaning cues and previous structure
It — (I get mixed up)	Recognizes the same word	I am confused. Start again	
It won't	Tries previous solution	Rejects	
went(?)	Tries correct sound 'e'	I do not recognize this word	There has been too much error
(I don't know that word)	Gives up	Appeals for help	No more ideas

Letter Identification

What letters does the child know? Which letters can he identify? It is not sufficient to say that he knows 'a few letters'. His tuition should take into account exactly what he knows. (This testing should take 5 to 10 minutes.)

• Test all letters, lower case and upper case. The large print alphabet that is printed in this book should be used. It could be removed from the book and mounted on a clipboard for this purpose. Ensure that the child reads *across* the lines so that the letters are treated in a random order.

• Use the Letter Identification Score Sheet (see Appendix). Mark A for an alphabetic response, S for sound, or W for word beginning similarly, and record the incorrect responses.
• Score as correct
— an alphabet name
— a sound that is acceptable for that letter
— a response which says '...*it begins like*...' giving a word for which that letter is the initial letter.

The scores given below apply when any one of these three criteria is used to mark a response correct. Obtain sub-totals for each kind of response, alphabetic, sound or word beginning similarly, and note down

- the child's preferred mode of identifying letters
- the letters a child confuses so that they can be kept apart in the teaching programme
- the unknown letters.

Administration
Use only the following questions to get the child to respond to the letters. *Do not ask only for sounds, or names:*

To introduce the task:
- What do you call these?
- Can you find some that you know?

Pointing to each letter:
- What is this one?

If a child does not respond:
Use one or more of these questions and try to avoid bias towards any one of them.
- Do you know its name?
- What sound does it make?
- Do you know a word that starts like that?

Then moving to other letters:
- What is this? And this?

If the child hesitates. start with the first letter of his name, and then go to the first line. Point to every letter in turn working across the lines. Use a masking card if necessary.

Following such testing, teaching should aim to improve the child's ability to distinguish letters one from another on any basis that works (not necessarily by letter-sound relationships). Expand the child's range of known letters allowing any distinction that works for that child. As more and more letters are controlled he becomes ready for systematic associations like alphabetic names and sound equivalents which can supplement the original association he chose.

The following tables show scores on Letter Identification as Stanine scores for two large samples of children aged five to seven years. (Stanines distribute scores according to the normal curve in nine groups from 1, a low score to 9, a high score (see Lyman, 1963). While Stanines can be used for normative test purposes that is not the reason for their use here. Stanines are used here so that progress can be compared across various tests which have different ranges of scores (i.e. when raw scores are not comparable). They allow one pupil's progress to be compared with another's or one pupil's scores at two points of time to be compared. As it is possible for young children to completely master this particular set of learning one would expect a child to move through the Stanine score range until he reached perfect scoring for the symbols of the alphabet.

For comparison choose the research group that best represents the group of children you will be testing.

Letter Identification scores are very sensitive to instructional procedures. The teaching of letter-sound relationships will result in most responses being sounds rather than names, and the whole set of letters may be learned earlier than under a different method of

Research Group	Letter Identification (Normalised Scores — Stanine Groups)									
320 urban children aged 5:0 - 7:0 in 1968	Stanine group	1	2	3	4	5	6	7	8	9
	Test score	—	0	1-7	8-25	26-47	48-52	53	54	—
282 urban children aged 6:0 - 7:3 in 1978	Stanine group	1	2	3	4	5	6	7	8	9
	Test score	0-13	14-28	29-43	44-49	50-52	53	—	54	—

Reliability:　100 urban children aged 6:0, 0.97, split-half, (Clay, 1966).
Validity:　Correlation with Word Reading for 100 children at 6:0, 0.85, (Clay, 1966).

A	F	K	P	W	Z
B	H	O	J	U	
C	Y	L	Q	M	
D	N	S	X	I	
E	G	R	V	T	
a	f	k	p	w	z
b	h	o	j	u	a
c	y	l	q	m	
d	n	s	x	i	
e	g	r	v	t	g

instruction. The 1968 sample of New Zealand children of mixed race was slower to learn Letter Identification responses than another sample tested in 1972.

Concepts About Print

A check (5 to 10 minutes) should be made on significant concepts about printed language. Some of these are: the front of the book, that print (not the picture) tells the story, what is a letter? what is a word? what is the first letter in a word? big and little letters, the function of the space, uses of punctuation (fullstop, question mark, talking marks).

Do not assume that verbal explanation has taught the eyes to locate, recognise and use this information.

The 'Concepts About Print' tests are entitled *Sand* (Clay, 1972), and *Stones* (Clay, 1979), and can be used with the 'new entrant' or the 'non-reader' because the child is asked to help the examiner by pointing to certain features as the examiner reads the book. Five-year-old children have some fun and little difficulty with the test items. The test reflects changes in reading skill during the first year of instruction but is of less significance in the subsequent years for children who make average progress. For problem readers confusions about these arbitrary conventions of our written language code tend to persist.

'Concepts About Print' has proved to be a sensitive indicator of one group of behaviours which support reading acquisition. As non-readers become readers changes occur in 'Concepts About Print' scores. The test is able to capture changes over time in an early intervention programme. 'Concepts About Print' has been translated and used with Danish, and Spanish-speaking children. The interest in 'Concepts About Print' has resulted in it being lifted from its position as a subtest in a wide-ranging survey designed to monitor changes in a complex set of reading behaviours and it has been expected to stand alone as some indicator of 'readiness' or reading progress. I do not like to see it reduced to a mere assessment device when it can be such a valuable guide for the teacher about one aspect, but only one aspect, of learning during the early stages of reading acquisition.

Administration

The tasks present a standard situation within which the child can be observed. Try to retain a standard task but be flexible enough to communicate the task to the child.

Administer the items according to the instructions given. If the child fails item 10, items 12 to 14 are likely to be failed and can be given at the discretion of the examiner. However, items 15 to 24 should be administered to all children. If items 12 to 14 are omitted you should still read the story on those pages to the child.

The instructions for the administration and scoring of this test have been printed on pages 28 and 29.

Research Group	Concepts About Print (Normalised Scores — Stanine Groups)									
320 urban children aged 5:0-7:0 in 1968	**Stanine score**	1	2	3	4	5	6	7	8	9
	Test score	0	1-4	5-7	8-11	12-14	15-17	18-20	21-22	23-24
282 urban children aged 6:0-7:3 in 1978	**Stanine score**	1	2	3	4	5	6	7	8	9
	Test score	0-9	10-11	12-13	14-16	17-18	19	20-21	22	23-24

Reliability: 40 urban children aged 5:0 to 7:0 in 1968, 0.95, KR (Clay, 1970).
56 kindergarten children in Texas 1978.
Test-retest reliability coefficients 0.73-0.89
Corrected split-half coefficients 0.84-0.88   (Day and Perkins, 1979)

Validity: Correlation with Word Reading for 100 children at 6:0, 0.79 (Clay, 1966)

Concepts About Print Test

Administration and scoring

Before starting, thoroughly familiarise yourself with this test. Use the exact wording given below in each demonstration. (Read the instructions from the printed text for each administration.)

Say to the child, :'*I'm going to read you this story but I want you to help me.*'.

Cover

Item 1	Test:	For orientation of book. Pass the booklet to the child holding the book vertically by outside edge, spine towards the child.
	Say:	'*Show me the front of this book.*'
	Score:	1 point for the correct response.

Pages 2/3

Item 2	Test:	Concept that print, not picture, carries the message.
	Say:	'*I'll read this story. You help me. Show me where to start reading. Where do I begin to read?*'
	Read the text.	
	Score:	1 for print. 0 for picture.

Pages 4/5

Item 3	Test:	For directional rules.
	Say:	'*Show me where to start.*'
	Score:	1 for top left.
Item 4	Say:	'*Which way do I go?*'
	Score:	1 for left to right.
Item 5	Say:	'*Where do I go after that?*'
	Score:	1 for return sweep to left.

(Score items 3-5 if all movements are demonstrated in one response.)

Item 6	Test:	Word by word pointing.
	Say:	'*Point to it while I read it.*' (Read slowly, but fluently.)
	Score:	1 for exact matching.

Page 6

Item 7	Test:	Concept of first and last.
	Read the text.	
	Say:	'*Show me the first part of the story.*' '*Show me the last part.*'
	Score:	1 point if BOTH are correct in any sense, i.e. applied to the whole text or a line, a word or a letter.

Page 7

Item 8	Test:	Inversion of picture.
	Say:	'*Show me the bottom of the picture*' (slowly and deliberately).
	Score:	(Do NOT mention upside-down.) 1 for verbal explanation, OR, for pointing to top of page, OR, for turning the book around and pointing appropriately.

Pages 8/9

Item 9	Test:	Response to inverted print.
	Say:	'*Where do I begin?*' '*Which way do I go?*' '*Where do I go after that?*'
	Score:	1 for beginning with 'The' (**Sand**), or 'I' (**Stones**), and moving right to left across the lower and then the upper line. OR 1 for turning the book around and moving left to right in the conventional manner.
	Read the text now.	

Pages 10/11

Item 10	Test:	Line sequence.
	Say:	'*What's wrong with this?*' (Read immediately the bottom line first, then the top line. Do NOT point.)
	Score:	1 for comment on line order.

Pages 12/13

Item 11	Test:	A left page is read before a right page.
	Say:	'*Where do I start reading?*'
	Score:	1 point for left page indication.
Item 12	Test:	Word sequence
	Say:	'*What's wrong on this page?*' (Point to the page number 12 — NOT the text.)
	Read the text slowly as if it were correct.	
	Score:	1 point for comment on either error.

Item 13 Test: Letter order.

Say: *'What's wrong on this page?'* (Point to the page number 13 — NOT the text.)

Read the text slowly as if it were correct.

Score: 1 point for any ONE re-ordering of letters that is noticed and explained.

Pages 14/15

Item 14 Test: Re-ordering letters within a word.

Say: *'What's wrong with the writing on this page?'*

Read the text slowly as if it were correct.

Score: 1 point for ONE error noticed.

Item 15 Test: Meaning of a question mark.

Say: *'What's this for?'* (Point to or trace the question mark with a finger or pencil.)

Score: 1 point for explanation of function or name.

Pages 16/17

Test: Punctuation.

Read the text.

Say: *'What's this for?'*

Item 16 Point to or trace with a pencil, the fullstop (period).

Item 17 Point to or trace with a pencil, the comma.

Item 18 Point to or trace with a pencil, the quotation marks.

Item 19 Test: Capital and lower-case correspondence.

Say: *'Find a little letter like this.'*

Sand: Point to capital T and demonstrate by pointing to an upper case T and a lower case t if the child does not succeed.
Stones: As above for S and s.

Say: *'Find a little letter like this.'*

Sand: Point to capital M, H in turn.

Stones: Point to capital T, B in turn.

Score: **Sand:** 1 point if BOTH Mm and Hh are located.
Stones: 1 point if BOTH Tt and Bb are located.

Pages 18/19

Item 20 Test: Reversible words.

Read the text.

Say: *'Show me was.'*
'Show me no.'

Score: 1 point for BOTH correct.

Page 20

Ensure you have two pieces of light card (13 x 5cm) that the child can hold and slide easily over the line of text to block out words and letters. To start, lay the cards on the page but leave all print exposed. Open the cards out between each question asked.

Item 21 Test: Letter concepts.

Say: *'This story says* (**Sand**) *"The waves splashed in the hole"* (or (**Stones**) *"The stone rolled down the hill"). I want you to push the cards across the story like this until all you can see is* (deliberately with stress) *just one letter.'* (Demonstrate the movement of the cards but do not do the exercise.)

Say: *'Now show me two letters.'*

Score: 1 point if BOTH are correct.

Item 22 Test: Word concept.

Say: *'Show me just one word.'*
'Now show me two words.'

Score: 1 point if BOTH are correct.

Item 23 Test: First and last letter concepts.

Say: *'Show me the first letter of a word.'*

'Show me the last letter of a word.'

Score: 1 point if BOTH are correct.

Item 24 Test: Capital letter concepts.

Say: *'Show me a capital letter.'*

Score: 1 point if correct.

Scoring Standards

Item	Pass	Score
1	Front of book.	
2	Print (not picture).	
3	Points top left at 'I took...' (Sand); 'I walked. . .' (Stones).	
4	Moves finger left to right on any line.	
5	Moves finger from the right-hand end of a higher line to the left-hand end of the next lower line, or moves down the page.	
6	Word by word matching.	
7	Both concepts must be correct, but may be demonstrated on the whole text or on a line, word or letter.	
8	Verbal explanation, or pointing to top of page, or turning the book around and pointing appropriately.	
9	Score for beginning with 'The' and moving right to left across the lower line and then the upper line, OR, turning the book around and moving left to right in the conventional movement pattern.	
10	Any explanation which implies that line order is altered.	
11	Says or shows that a left page precedes a right page.	
12	Notices at least one change of word order.	
13	Notices at least one change in letter order.	
14	Notices at least one change in letter order.	
15	Says 'Question mark', or 'A question', or 'Asks something'.	
16	Says 'Full stop', 'Period', or 'It tells you when you've said enough' or 'It's the end'.	
17	Says 'A little stop', or 'A rest', or 'A comma'.	
18	Says 'That's someone talking', 'Talking', 'Speech marks', 'Print' (from computers).	
19	Locates two capital and lower case pairs.	
20	Points correctly to both *was* and *no*.	
21	Locates one letter and two letters on request.	
22	Locates one word and two words on request.	
23	Locates both a first and a last letter.	
24	Locates one capital letter.	

Age Expectations For Items

(Age at which 50 percent of average European children pass an item, Clay, 1970)

Age Item	5:0	5:6	6:0	6:6	7:0	Item	5:0	5:6	6:0	6:6	7:0
1		x				13				x	
2	x					14					x
3		x				15				x	
4		x				16					x
5		x				17					x
6		x				18					x
7		x				19			x		
8		x				20			x		
9		x				21		x			
10		x				22			x		
11		x				23				x	
12				x		24				x	

Interpretation of scores

Score items as instructed on pages 28 and 30. Use one of the tables on page 27 to convert these scores to a Stanine score for New Zealand children only.

Choose the first table if you are assessing five-year-olds, or if the average Stanine score of 5 seems to fit with average progress in your school. Choose the second table if you are assessing six-year-olds, or if your children tend to move more quickly in this test area.

A Stanine score is a normalised standard score of nine units, with 1 a low score and 9 a high score. An individual child's Stanine score indicates his status relative to all children in the age group 5:0 to 7:0. It is useful to contrast a particular child's scores after an interval to reflect progress.

It is also useful for a school to build up its own table of Stanine scores. (Lyman, 1963.)

As the 'Concepts About Print' are a limited set of information which can be learned in the first two years of school, young children will test low early in their schooling and their Stanine score should increase as their reading improves.

However the test's greatest value is diagnostic. Items should uncover concepts to be learned or confusions to be untangled. For remedial purposes examine the child's performance and teach the unknown concepts. The items are not in a strict difficulty sequence, but some indication of difficulty is given by the 'Age Expectations for Items' table which gives the age at which average children passed each item. (However, such data will be very dependent on the teaching programme and method-emphasis used in any particular school.)

Word Tests

Standardised word tests are based on the principle of sampling from the child's reading vocabulary. They cannot be reliable until the child has acquired sufficient vocabulary to make sampling a feasible strategy.

For early identification a different approach is required. Word lists can be compiled from the high frequency words in the reading materials that are adopted. The principle here is a sampling from the high frequency words of that restricted corpus that the child has had the opportunity to learn. The following test works well for children who are using the New Zealand 'Ready to Read' series (1963).

'Ready to Read' Word Test

It should be noted that any test of first year instruction must be closely linked to that instruction. *The most frequently occurring words* in whatever basic reading texts are being used will probably provide a satisfactory source of test items.

It was found for Auckland children that a small list of 15 words systematically sampled from the 45 most frequently occurring words in the twelve little books of the New Zealand 'Ready to Read' series (1963) was a very good instrument for ranking or grouping children during *the first year* of instruction and for retarded readers in the second year (Clay, 1966). This test, which takes about two minutes to administer, can be removed and mounted on a clipboard for easy administration.

Administration

Ask a child to read *one* list. Give List A *or* List B *or* List C. Help the child with the practice word if necessary and never score it. Do not help with any other words and do not use the list for teaching. Use alternate lists for retesting.

Use of the Test

The score will indicate the extent to which a child is accumulating a reading vocabulary of the most frequently used words in the *Ready to Read* series (1963) during his first year at school.

The scores may be used for ranking or grouping children (together with teachers' observations recorded for book reading). Successive tests will indicate whether a progressive change is occurring in the child's reading skill.

Score

The following table shows scores on the *Ready to Read* Word Test as Stanine scores for a large sample of children aged five to seven years. (Stanines distribute scores according to the normal curve in nine groups from 1, the lowest, to 9.) It is possible for children to completely master this learning. One would therefore expect a child to move through the Stanine score range until he reached perfect scoring.

What the Test does not do:

• It does not give a reading age.
• It does not discriminate between better readers after one year of instruction. On the contrary it groups them together.
• Differences of less than three score points are not sufficiently reliable to support any decisions about the child's progress, without other evidence.
• It does not sample a child's reading skill if he is working beyond the level of the first twelve books of the *Ready to Read* series (1963).

Research Group	'Ready to Read' Word Test (Normalized Scores — Stanine Groups)								
320 urban children aged 5:0-7:0 in 1968	**Stanine group**	1	2	3	4	5	6	7	8	9
	Test score	0	0	1	2-5	6-12	13-14	—	15	—
282 urban children aged 6:0-7:3 in 1978	**Stanine group**	1	2	3	4	5	6	7	8	9
	Test score	0-1	2-5	6-9	10-12	13-14	—	15	—	—

Reliability: 100 urban children aged 6:0, 0.90, KR (Clay, 1966).
Validity: Correlation was 0.90 for Word Test at 6:0 with Schonell R1 at 7:0 for 87 children.

Other Reading Tests

Once the child who entered school at five years has a reading level of 6:0 to 6:6 several standardised tests can be applied. A word test, like the Schonell R1, the Southgate Group Reading Test or the Burt Word Reading Test (NZCER, 1981) will not describe the child's integrated system of reading behaviour because this can only be observed on continuous text. It will rank the child in relation to other children on reading vocabulary.

The Schonell test was used in many New Zealand studies because research clearly demonstrated that the score for the Word Test of 15 words (described in the last section) could be added to the score for the first 30 words of the Schonell R1 test to give a combined score which was psychometrically a good measure of reading of New Zealand children between five and seven years. This is now replaced by the newly standardised Burt Word Reading Test. This test describes children's level of attainment as a range rather than a reading age, allowing for the variations that occur in testing. In most countries there will be word tests of reading commonly used in schools which can be added to the test battery to provide normative comparisons.

On the other hand, a paragraph reading test, like the Neale Analysis of Reading Ability (1958), will permit observations of the child's ongoing behaviour, in a situation which is standard and which is graded in difficulty. A teacher who has thought about the reading process can extract much more information about the child's system of operating on cues in reading from a running record on a paragraph reading test than is yielded only by the test scores on this test.

For children whose reading level is above the average after two years of instruction, the Gap Reading Comprehension Test (McLeod, 1965) can be used as a paragraph reading test with groups. It provides some evidence of the children's use of meaning and grammatical structure cues.

Writing

Examine examples of the child's writing behaviour. Does he have good letter formation? How many letter forms does he use? Does he have a stock of words which he can construct from memory with the letters correctly sequenced? What are they?

A poor writing vocabulary may indicate that, despite all his efforts to read, a child is in fact taking very little notice of visual differences in print. He requires an all-out effort to induce more writing behaviour to correct for his faulty visual perception. In learning, the hand *and* eye support and supplement each other, organising the first visual discriminations. Only later does the eye become a solo agent and learning become faster than at the hand-eye learning stage.

LIST A	LIST B	LIST C
Practice Word	Practice Word	Practice Word
the	said	is

I	and	Father
Mother	to	come
are	will	for
here	look	a
me	he	you
shouted	up	at
am	like	school
with	in	went
car	where	get
children	Mr	we
help	going	they
not	big	ready
too	go	this
meet	let	boys
away	on	please

	A Language Level	B Message Quality	C Directional Principles
Not yet satisfactory	1-4	1-4	1-4
Probably satisfactory	5-6	5-6	5-6

Writing samples

A rating technique for early attempts to write stories
Use this kind of appraisal for the early reading stage. Take three samples of the child's stories on consecutive days or for three successive weeks and rate them for language level, message quality and directional features. (One sample is not sufficiently reliable for this evaluation technique.)

Language level
Record the number of the highest level of linguistic organisation used by the child.

1 Alphabetic (letters only).
2 Word (any recognisable word).
3 Word group (any two-word phrase).
4 Sentence (any simple sentence).
5 Punctuated story (of two or more sentences).
6 Paragraphed story (two themes).

Message quality
Record the number below for the best description of the child's sample.

1 He has a concept of signs (uses letters, invents letters, uses punctuation).
2 He has a concept that a message is conveyed.
3 A message is copied.
4 Repetitive use of sentence patterns like 'Here is a . . .'
5 Attempts to record own ideas.
6 Successful composition.

Directional principles
Record the number of the highest rating for which there is no error in the sample of the child's writing.

1 No evidence of directional knowledge.
2 Part of the directional pattern is known:
   Either start top left
   Or move left to right
   Or return down left.
3 Reversal of the directional pattern (right to left and return down right).

4 Correct directional pattern.
5 Correct directional pattern and spaces between words.
6 Extensive text without any difficulties of arrangement and spacing of text.

A test of writing vocabulary

A test of writing vocabulary, constructed by Susan E. Robinson (1973) was included in the test battery of her research on predicting early reading progress. Hildreth (1964) and de Hirsch et al (1966) had suggested that writing behaviour was a good indicator of a child's knowledge of letters, and of left to right sequencing behaviour. In writing words letter by letter the child must recall not only the configuration but also the details. Children's written texts are a good source of information about a child's visual discrimination of print for as the child learns to print words, hand and eye support and supplement each other to organise the first visual discriminations.

A test was constructed where the child was encouraged to write down all the words he knew how to write, starting with his own name and including basic vocabulary and words personal to the child. This simple test was both reliable (i.e. a child tended to score at a similar level when retested two weeks later) and valid in the sense that it had a high relationship with word reading scores.

The distribution of scores changes markedly with age when a group of children aged five-and-a-half are compared with two groups of six-year-olds (page 37). In the first year of school there is probably a high degree of interdependence between reading words and writing words. Writing ability and word reading ability may both be the result of many kinds of experience with letters, numbers, words, stories and drawings which have enabled the child to learn many things about print. It should not be assumed from this that success in the first years of learning to read would be assured by simply teaching children to write words.

Administration and scoring
Give the child a blank piece of paper and a pencil and then say '*I want to see how many words you can write. Can you write your name?*' (Start ten minute timing here.)

• If the child says 'No', ask him if he knows any single letter or two letter words.

'Do you know how to write is? to? I? or a?'

and then suggest other words he may know how to write (see below).

• If the child says 'Yes' say

'Write your name for me.'

When the child finishes say

'Good. Now think of all the words you know how to write and write them all down for me.'

Give the child up to 10 minutes to write words he knows. When he stops writing, or when he needs prompting, suggest words that he might know how to write.

'Do you know how to write I or a?'

'Do you know how to write is or to?'

Go through a list of words that the child would have met in his reading books: child's name, I, a, is, in , am, to, come, like, see, the, my, we, and, at, here, on, up, look, go, this, it, me.

Continue for 10 minutes or until the child's writing vocabulary is exhausted. Very able children need little prompting but sometimes it is necessary to suggest a category of words.

The following list of questions suggest some examples.

'Do you know how to write any children's names?

'Do you know how to write things you do?

'Do you know how to write the names of any animals?

'Do you know how to write things in the house (or the kitchen)?

'Do you know how to write things to ride on (or in)?

'Do you know how to write things to eat?

'Do you know how to write . . .?

'Do you know how to write . . .?

Scoring

Each word completed accurately is marked as correct. If the child accidentally writes a word that is correct but reads it as another word or does not know what it is, that word is scored as an error. Words written in mirror image are scored as correct only if the child actually wrote them in the correct sequence. Groups of words such as look, looks, looked, looking, and sat, fat, mat, hat, are allowed as separate words.

Attainment

Some children cannot produce their own names. Half of the children in Robinson's study (1973) aged 5:6 could not write more than four to seven words. Only four children at this age wrote more than 13 words. The results for children aged 6:0 were far higher, the mean score for two samples being 27 and 30. Even with the 10 minute time limit the writing vocabulary of able children was by no means exhausted. One child wrote 79 words in ten minutes.

A developmental record of a child's progress may be kept by taking an inventory of writing vocabulary at several points in time — at entry, after six months and after one year. In the examples on the next page for Ross, Nicola and Joanne the progress of each child is evident even though they are at three different levels of attainment.

Stanine scores for one group of children are provided.

Research Group	Writing Vocabulary (Normalised Scores — Stanine Groups)								
282 urban children aged 6:0-7:3 in 1978	Stanine group	1	2	3	4	5	6	7	8	9
	Test score	0-13	14-19	20-28	29-35	36-45	46-55	56-70	71-80	81-

Reliability: 34 urban children aged 5:6 in 1972, (Robinson, 1973) 0.97, test-retest.
Validity: Correlation with reading; 50 urban children aged 5:6 in 1972, (Robinson, 1973) 0.82.

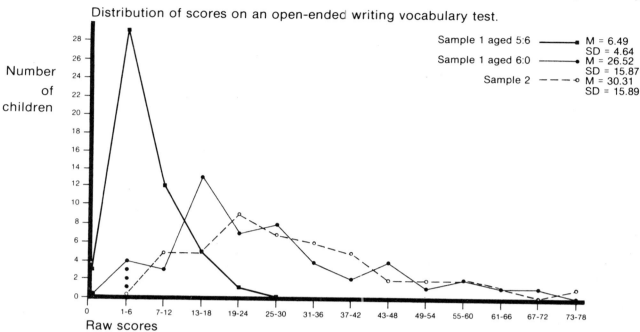

Distribution of scores on an open-ended writing vocabulary test.

Sample 1 aged 5:6 ████■ M = 6.49 SD = 4.64
Sample 1 aged 6:0 ─────● M = 26.52 SD = 15.87
Sample 2 ─ ─ ─○ M = 30.31 SD = 15.89

Time 1   ROSS B

Time 2   ROSS BELL
             I LS PU t O P M G C

Time 1   Joanne   I a Ann up in going and
             the they   Here where to at
             mother Father   go my Peter Sally
             we me ch ho

Time 2   Joanne
             at   nothon on michael
             I a is put   going
             nill can Too   three He
             this So go up LookBook
             to come go Came   same
             we He   yefne hareaBoutd red
             See   in down thalk thank-
             out ann and Pin into Big you
             Car Bill and Father mother   am
             pall home Peter house Sally
             mr mRs miss Little School
             Silly Jenny

Time 1   Nicola
             I a si
             KIM R A O BK
                I MN

Time 2   Nicola
             the
             this
             is
             a
             I
             it
             to
             up
             In
             INtO
             on
             we
             he
             the
             cr
             For
             mummy
             DADDY
             little
             A

A dictation test*

Simple sentences can be used as a dictation test. The child is given credit for every *sound* that he writes correctly, even though the word may not be correct. The scores give some indication of the child's ability to analyse the word he hears or says and to find some way of recording the sounds he hears as letters.

Administration

Say to the child:

'*I am going to read you a story. When I have read it through once I will read it again very slowly so that you can write down the words in the story.*'

Read the test sentences at normal speed:

'*Some of the words are hard.*
Say them slowly and think how you would write them.'

Dictate slowly. When the child comes to a problem word, say:

'*You say it slowly. How would you start to write it . . . What can you hear?*'

Then add:

'*What else can you hear?*'

If the child cannot complete the word say:

'*We'll leave that word. The next one is . . .*'

Point to where to write the next word if this helps the child.

Support the child with comments like these to keep the child working at the task.

There are five alternative dictation tests with one or two sentences. When retesting it is advisable to use an alternate form. The tests are listed on the following page.

Recording

Write the text below the child's version.

hm	skol	b
him	school	big

Tests and scoring

Score one point for each *sound* (phoneme) the child has analysed that is numbered one to 37 below and total out of 37.

Changes in letter order

Where the child has made a change in letter order, take one mark off for that word. For example:

$\frac{ma}{am}$ 2 – 1 = 1 $\frac{gonig}{going}$ 5 – 1 = 4

Alternatives accepted

Alternatives are accepted when the *sound* analysis is a useful one. For example:

skool	tace
school	take

Additions and omissions

1 If a letter does not have a number underneath it in the scoring standards on the next page then it receives *no* score even if a preceding letter is omitted. For example:

$\frac{tody}{today}$ = 3

2 Additions do not affect scoring as long as numbered letters are included. For example:

$\frac{todae}{today}$ = 4

Make some notes about:

- any sequencing errors
- omission of sounds
- unusual use of space on the page
- unusual placement of letters within words.

These may provide teaching points later in the child's programme.

* Susan Robinson and Barbara Watson devised and used these tests in the reading recovery programme, where they proved to be useful indicators of the child's ability to go from his analysis of sounds in spoken words to written forms for representing these sounds. In that sense this is not a true dictation or spelling test.

Administration and scoring
Select one of the following alternate Forms; A, B, C, D or E.

Form A

```
I   h a v e   a   b i g   d o g   a t       h o m e .
1   2 3 4     5   6 7 8   9 10 11  12 13     14 15 16

T o d a y  I  a m       g o i n g       t o   t a k e   h i m
17 18 19 20  21 22      23 24 25 26 27      28 29 30    31 32 33

t  o   s c h oo l .
34 35  36 37
```

Form B

```
M u m   h a s   g o n e   u p   t o  t h e   s h o p .
1 2 3   4 5 6   7 8 9     10 11 12 13 14 15  16 17 18

S h e   w i l l   g e t   m i l k   a n d
19 20   21 22 23  24 25 26 27 28 29 30 31 32 33

b r e a d .
34 35 36  37
```

Form C

```
I   c a n   s e e   t h e   r e d
1   2 3 4   5 6     7 8     9 10 11

b o a t   t h a t   w e   a r e   g o i n g
12 13 14  15 16 17  18 19 20 21   22 23 24 25 26

t  o   h a v e   a   r i d e   i n .
27 28  29 30 31  32  33 34 35  36 37
```

Form D

```
T h e   b u s   i s   c o m i n g .   I t
1 2 3   4 5     6 7   8 9 10 11 12 13  14 15

w i l l   s t o p   h e r e   t o   l e t   m e
16 17 18  19 20 21 22 23 24 25 26 27 28 29 30 31 32

g e t   o n .
33 34 35 36 37
```

Form E

```
T h e   b o y   i s   r i d i n g   h i s   b i k e .
1 2 3   4 5 6   7 8   9 10 11 12    13 14 15 16 17 18

H e   c a n   g o   v e r y   f a s t   o n   i t .
19 20 21 22 23 24 25 26 27 28 29 30 31 32 33 34 35 36 37
```

Research Group	Dictation Test (Normalized scores — Stanine Groups)								
282 urban children aged 6:0 - 7:3 in 1978	**Stanine group**	1	2	3	4	5	6	7	8	9
	Test score	0-3	4-9	10-17	18-27	28-31	32-35	36-37	—	—

Writing a story

An older child who can write 50 or more words is too competent for the Writing Vocabulary Test. He should be encouraged to write a story of several sentences or paragraphs (with as little help as possible) to provide a basis for grouping children's stories from say A to E. To assess change over time an earlier record for one child can be compared with a later one to estimate progress.

Spelling

Older children can be given a spelling test. The useful information on these tests is the evidence that is provided by watching the child at work and noting his strengths (words known, strategies that work, directional control and so on). The incorrect responses provide evidence of gaps, confusions or of interfering strategies. The test score or spelling age is information of lesser value. Sources used in New Zealand have been:

• Arvidson Spelling List (NZCER, 1960)
• NZCER Basic Word List (Elley, 1969)
• The Spell-Write Word List (NZCER, 1982).

4 Summarising the Diagnostic Survey Results

The Diagnostic Summary brings all the test results together. It describes the child's strengths and weaknesses, and indicates the strategies that are used and those that are not used.

From the detailed information which the survey yields it has proved useful to summarise the results under the headings listed on the Diagnostic Survey Summary Sheet (page 111) as follows.

Book reading
Analysis of errors to show what cues the child uses.

Test results
Analysis of strategies used by the child.
  Useful strategies on text.
  Problem strategies on text.
  Useful strategies with words.
  Problem strategies with words.
  Useful strategies with letters and sounds.
  Problem strategies with letters and sounds.

Case summary
Using only the evidence you have been reporting describe in a few lines the child's current way of responding. Point out what he can and cannot do on text reading and text writing. Indicate how his strategies on word and letter levels help or hinder his getting messages from text. The starting point of your programme should arise naturally out of this statement.

Looking for Strategies

There are several reasons for this approach to summarising the Survey.

• Language is organised hierarchically on several levels. Three have been selected here — letter, word, and text (a general term to stand for phrase, sentence or larger text).
• It has been argued that although the reader appears to have stored many items of knowledge he has also learned strategies for storing or filing this information, for retrieving it, and for linking or cross-referencing one kind of information with another kind.

Good observation rather than modern linguistic theory led a talented reading clinician Grace Fernald in 1943 to formulate statements about the relationships of letters, words and texts in reading.

'Groups of words must be the focus of attention in reading. Attending to the words as separate units, as in word-by-word reading loses important meanings. The meaning of a word can vary with the group in which it occurs or, in another way, a group of words has a certain meaning.

The sentence is the context in which the *meaning of the word group* is confirmed.

The known word is the unit at which level the precision of the word group is usually confirmed.

For the unknown, unfamiliar, forgotten or misperceived word the reader's attention must go to clusters of letters or even to individual letters but whether these are right or not must be confirmed at the level of the word unit.'

She insisted therefore that in writing the word should always be written as a unit, and in reading words should always be used in context.

The way of summarising the survey results adopted in the summary sheet is deficient in that it does not allow for the description and detection of strengths and weaknesses in those strategies which relate one level of linguistic organisation to another. We do not yet know much about such strategies.

Some examples of what is meant by reading strategies are given in case reports for:

• Mary at 6:0 — Early Reading.
• Paul at 6:9 — First Reading Books.
• Brian at 7:3 — Use of Graded Paragraphs.

The questions listed in the next section helped some teachers to describe the reading strategies that young children use.

Useful Strategies on Text

Look at the Running Record of book reading where the child is performing adequately (90 to 100 percent accuracy) and try to find some evidence of how effectively he works with the sequences of cues. Also look at 'Concepts About Print Test' items. Use these questions as a guide to your analysis of the records.

Location and movement
Does he control directional movement?
— left to right?
— top to bottom?
— return sweep?
Does he locate particular cues in print? Which cues?
Does he read word by word? If so, is this a new achievement (+) or an old habit (–)?

Language
Does he control language well?
Does he read for meaning?
Does he control book language?
Does he have a good memory for text?
Does he read for the precise message?

Behaviour at difficulties
Does he seek help?
Does he try again?
Does he search for further cues? How?
Note unusual behaviours.

Error substitutions
Do the error substitutions the child uses make sense with the previous text?
(Meaning)
Do they continue an acceptable sentence in English?
(Structure)
Could they occur in grammar for that sentence, up to that word?
Are some of the letters the same? (Visual or graphic cues.)

Self-correction
Does he return to the beginning of the line?
Does he return back a few words?
Does he repeat the word only?
Does he read on to the end of the line (a difficult and confusing strategy for young readers)?
Does he repeat only the initial sound of a word?
Note unusual behaviour.

Cross-checking strategies
At an early stage of text reading —
    does he ignore discrepancies?

does he check language with movement?
does he check language with visual cues?
does he try to make language, movement and visual cues line up?

Useful Strategies on Words

Check 'Concepts About Print' (CAP), Text reading, Writing Vocabulary, Dictation Test, and Word tests.

The visual features of words
On CAP recognises line rearrangement.
On CAP recognises word rearrangement.
On CAP recognises that the first and last letters are rearranged.
On CAP recognises that the medial letters are rearranged.

On text can attend to detail.
Responds to initial letters.
Responds to initial and final letters.
Relates to some prior visual or writing experience of that word.

On Writing Vocabulary the child knows some words in every detail.

The sounds of words
Can hear the individual words in a sentence.
Can articulate words slowly.
Can break up words into sounds (as in a dictated sentence).
Attempts to write new words using a sound analysis.
Builds a consonant framework for a new word.
Knows that vowels are difficult and works at them.
Re-reads what he has written, carefully.

Useful Strategies on Letters

Check 'Concepts About Print', Text reading, Letter Identification, Writing Vocabulary, Dictation Test and Word tests.

Movement
Does the child form (write) some letters easily?
Does he form many letters without a copy?

Visual
Which letters can he identify?
How does he identify them?
Which letters does he use as cues in reading?
Could he detect an error because of a mismatch of letters?
(Which letters were difficult?)
(Which letters were confused one with another?)

Sounds
How does a child attempt a word in the Dictation Test?
Does he articulate it slowly?
Can he isolate the first sound of a word that he hears?
Can he give other words that start with the same sound?

Case Summaries

Mary aged 6:0
Initial testing: 4.5.77
Initial status: Early reading — Caption Books.

1   *Book reading*
Mary read three Caption Books: *I am big* (seen). *The Bear Family* (seen) and *I am little* (unseen) with 94, 87, 75 percent accuracy and 0:3, 1:5, 0:8 self-correction rates. She read half of a red level supplementary, *Wake Up* (Star 1₃) which was not scored.

2   *Test results*
Mary's score on Letter Identification was 34/54, on Concepts About Print was 13/24, on the Word tests was 3/15 and 0/30, on Writing Vocabulary was 2 and on the Dictation Test was 8/37.

3   *Useful strategies on text*
Mary uses fluent book language.
She moves across the print from left to right with return sweep.

Problem strategies on text
Mary's fluent language response overrides visual and locating cues.
Under the tester's monitoring she *can* locate word by word and *can* attend to the words she knows in print (*I, am, is , here*), but when she works independently her language response is too fluent to allow any integration of cues.
Her self-correction rates are low.
She does not attend to letter cues. Her miscues had zero graphic correspondence.

4   *Useful strategies on words*
Mary recognised *I, here, am* in isolation.
She wrote the sentence:

I si a May (for *I am Mary*)

She analysed some initial sounds (have, big, home) on the dictation test.

Problem strategies on words
Mary does not attend to words while reading unless asked to 'Look carefully and read with your finger'. Locating in print and coordinating finger and speech in word-by-word reading is a difficult coordination for her to make.

5   *Useful strategies on letters*
Mary identified 34/54 letters by name.
She knows some sound-to-letter relationships.

Problem strategies on letters
Mary confuses 15 letters:

I	F	I	j	q	g	i	r	b	h	k	j	b	b	O
L	E	T	f	u	y	l	q	d	n	x	i	p	g	Q

Diagnostic summary
Mary has made some progress with the use of visual cues but her fluent language overrides visual cues and prevents word-by-word reading. Discrepancies do not signal to her to recheck and self-correct.

Paul aged 6:9
Initial testing: 9.8.77
Initial status: First Readers

1   *Book reading*
Paul read *Early in the Morning* Red 1 Level (seen) with 98 percent accuracy and 0:1 self-corrections and *The Lazy Pig* (PM 1j) with 79 percent accuracy and 1:3 self-corrections.

2   *Test results*
Paul's score on Letter Identification was 31/54, on Concepts About Print was 19/24, on the Word tests was 3/15 and 4/30, on Writing Vocabulary was 7 and on the Dictation Test was 11/37.

3   *Useful strategies on text*
Paul predicts meaningful language from picture clues with 1:1 matching, using some initial letter-to-sound knowledge. He self-corrects some mismatches and known words.

Problem strategies on text
His miscues have semantic and syntactic acceptability but not graphic acceptability. He is very distractable and often uses diversionary tactics to escape the reading task.

4 *Useful strategies on words*

He identified 3/15, and 4/30 words in isolation.
He wrote seven words.
He uses word knowledge in reading text.
He analyses some sounds within words.

Problem strategies on words

Recall of words, especially basic words, seems to be a difficult area.
Language overrides word knowledge in reading.

Child:	awake		woke
Text:	up	(5 x)	am

5 *Useful strategies on letters*

He identified 31/54 letter symbols by letter name.
He analyses initial sounds and some sounds within words.
He uses some initial letter-to-sound knowledge in reading.

Problem strategies on letters

He confused $\frac{n \ u \ x \ z \ E}{u \ y \ z \ x \ F}$ on Letter Identification and $\frac{W}{M}$ in writing.

Diagnostic summary

Paul has shown progress in component skills of reading but his age and habituated diversionary tactics, his difficulty in recalling sight words and his overriding language response in reading text have prevented any rapid reading progress.

Running Records with Older Readers

An analysis of error behaviour: Brian

The graded paragraphs of the Neale Analysis of Reading Ability (Form B) were administered to Brian, a boy aged 7:3 with very good reading strategies in his third year of instruction. In addition to standard scoring of the test this running record of reading behaviour was made by a second year Education student without training or experience in teaching. For the text of the paragraphs the reader is referred to Neale (1958).

Paragraph one

√ √ √ √ √ √
√ √ √ √ √ √
√ √ √ √ √ √ √ √
√ √ √ √ √ √

Running words	:	26
Accuracy	:	100%
Error rate	:	Nil
Self-correction rate	:	Nil
Repetition	:	Nil
Prompts	:	Nil
Comprehension	:	100%

Paragraph two

√ √ √ √ √
√ √ √ √ √
√ √ $\frac{h}{had}$ |had √ √
√ √ √ $\frac{n}{not}$ |not √ √
√ √ √ √ √ √
√ √ √ √ $\frac{h}{held}$ |held √
√ √ √ √ held √
√ √ $\frac{the}{-}$ |R|SC √ √ √
√ √ √ √

Running words	:	49
Accuracy	:	100%
Error rate	:	Nil
Self-correction rate	:	One
Repetition	:	Nil
Prompts	:	Nil
Comprehension	:	50%
Solving strategies	:	First letter sounding (h, n)

Paragraph three

√ √ √ √ √ √
√ √ √ $\frac{th}{theatre}$ |Told √ √ √
√ √ √ √ √ √ √ √ √
$\frac{w}{wore}$ |wore √ √ √ √ √
√ √ √ √ √ √ √
√ √ √ √ √ √ √
√ √ √ √ √ √ √

$\frac{√}{√ \text{like}}$ $\frac{a}{the}$ |R|SC $\frac{r}{required}$ |Asks |Told √√ $\frac{ch}{cheers}$ |cheers|

$\frac{grated}{greeted}$ √ √ √ √ √ √ √

√ √ √ √↓ $\frac{put}{but}$ |R|SC √ √ √

Running words | : | 72
Accuracy | : | 96%
Error rate | : | 1 in 24
Self-correction rate | : | 2 in 7
Repetition | : | Nil
Prompts | : | theatre, required
Comprehension | : | 25%
Solving strategies | : | Letter cues to self-correction (a/the)
| | Beginning and end (greeted, but)
| | First sound (th, ch, r, w)
| | Syntax acceptable, meaning not (grated)
| | Syntax and meaning both in error (put/but)

Prompts | : | mournful, proceeded, exhausted, imprisoned, cautiously, curiosity
Comprehension | : | 80%
Solving strategies | : | Beginning and end correct (cased, mounting, mysterious, courage, scarcely)
| | First letter always correct
| | Syllabic attack (nevertheless, in-, ab-, pro-, dar-)
| | Syntax + meaning + letter cues (distant for deserted (d-s-t))
| | Syntax + letter cues but not meaning (cased)

Scoring and analysis

This is provided on the table on page 46.

Descriptive comments

Brian read word by word, staccato, at a fast pace. He ignored punctuation and paused at difficult words and the end of lines, losing meaning and sense. Intonation was flat and even with little variation.

In correcting himself Brian went back to the previous word but not to the beginning of the sentence or line.

Brian used initial letters or clusters and last letters or clusters for cues. He did not use medial sounds, syllables or clusters as efficiently.

Recommendations

Although only seven years of age Brian has a reading age of nine years and this analysis of his reading of continuous text shows that two emphases typical of nine-year-old learning are required in Brian's programme. He could now develop a more consciously controlled syllabic attack, with attention to medial vowels and syllables. Meantime he should place more value on meaning by using punctuation cues, by phrasing, and by searching until the difficult word makes sense.

This may mean a temporary drop in fluency while syllabic attack and semantic checks are incorporated into his present patterns of reading behaviour.*

* The author is indebted to the careful observation of Maris O'Rourke for this case study.

Paragraph four

✓	✓	✓	✓	m / mournful	Asks / Told	✓	✓
✓	✓	✓		distant / deserted		cast-lay / castle	
✓	cased / ceased	✓	ab / abruptly	am | amb | ambrutli			✓
✓	✓	✓	✓	✓

✓	✓ ✓	never the less / nevertheless	✓	pro / proceeded	Asks / Told
c / cautiously	Told	✓ ✓ ✓ ✓ ✓	mysteries / mysterious	✓
	cowrige / courage	and with	SC	mountining / mounting
C / curiosity	Told	✓	✓	✓	✓	✓	✓

✓	sce ali / scarcely	dare / daring	SC	✓	✓	✓	✓
✓	✓	✓	✓	✓	✓	✓
✓	✓	✓	the / their	✓
✓	✓	✓	✓	✓	✓	e / exhausted	Told
✓	✓	✓	✓	✓	✓	✓	im / imprisoned	Asks / Told
✓	✓	✓	✓	✓	✓	✓	✓	✓

Running words | : | 92
Accuracy | : | 82.6%
Error rate | : | 1 in 5
Self-correction rate | : | 1 in 9
Repetition | : | Nil

From a Running Record of a Seven-Year-Old Using Tests from the Neale Analysis of Reading

Paragraph	One	Two	Three	Four
Running words	26	49	72	92
Accuracy	100%	100%	96%	83%
Error rate	nil	nil	1:24	1:5
Self-correction rate	nil	(one)	1:3	1:9
Repetition	nil	nil	nil	nil
Prompts	nil	nil	theatre, required	mourning proceeded exhausted imprisoned cautiously curiosity
Comprehension	100%	50%	25%	80%
Solving strategies	nil	first letters sounded (h,n)	1 letter cues (a/the) 2 beginning & end (greeted, but) 3 first sound (th, ch, r, w) 4 syntax acceptable, meaning not (grated) 5 syntax + meaning both in error (put, but)	1 beginning and end correct (cased mounting, mysterious, courage, scarcely) 2 first letter always correct 3 syllabic attack (nevertheless, in-, ab-, pro-, dar-) 4 syntax + meaning + letter cues (distant for deserted (d-s-t)) 5 syntax + letter cues but not meaning (cased)

PART TWO

READING RECOVERY: AN EARLY INTERVENTION PROGRAMME

A note of caution must be sounded. Most children (80 to 90 percent) do NOT require these detailed, meticulous and special reading recovery procedures *or any modification of them.* They will learn to read more pleasurably without them. For a few children individual and consistent tutoring with these special procedures introduced after one year of instruction may well prevent the development of a pattern of reading failure.

5 Organising to Prevent Reading Failure

The first essential of a satisfactory early intervention programme is to have a good reading instruction programme in the schools. Most children will learn to read in Junior class programmes which take individual needs and personal learning schedules into account. Against the background of a sound general programme it is possible to develop a strategy for reducing the numbers of children with reading difficulties. This involves a check on the age group at the end of the first year at school, a second chance programme for those who need it and specialist services for those whose problems persist.

At the beginning of schooling, when children enter formal instruction the foundations of all their future interactions with education are being laid. Children need to emerge from these years with a control of the language of instruction (and another language if they are fortunate) well on the way to becoming the kind of reader whose reading improves because he reads, and on the way to becoming a writer. These language arts are the tools needed by the child for further educational progress, particularly in an information age.

What happens to the five-year-olds who come into school? How are they grouped? When are they moved to another group? Or to a new class? What exactly happens about shifting groups of children from one class to another? Each school knows what it does, but there is no description of what everyone else does and no evaluation of one practice against another. It would be interesting to compare schools, noting differences in organisation and differences in the criteria used for moving children. We would find different solutions in schools of different sizes. For example, in a system with an admissions policy of continuous entry the growth rate of a district would make a difference. If one school has new entrants coming at the rate of a whole new class a month it is going to have different kinds of problems and different solutions for class organisation from a school where one class fills up in the first six months or in the first year. These questions are related to the quality of instruction given to the new entrants.

Countries decide on some arbitrary basis, for historical reasons, or custom, or convention, the age at which children start school. Once the large group of children is in a classroom then their lives will be different from what they would have been had they not come into formal education at that time. Simply bringing them into formal education, into a reception class, into developmental programmes changes the life opportunities for those children. Whatever the child has been able to learn before he comes to school, whatever his behaviours are, whatever

his response to his environment has been, it now goes through some transitions. The teacher in the reception class is trying to bring the children from those varied behaviours that they learned in their preschool years towards some behaviours shared with other children. The teacher is trying to encourage a transition from the behaviour that the child brings to school to some behaviour he can use in school on academic tasks. He may have limited language patterns and these have to be brought to something that can be worked on along with other children in a programme. He may be withdrawn, and his social behaviour may be brought to the point where he can work with a group.

Because we invite children into formal education we must give up the idea that 'they ripen and mature so that after a while they begin to read'. This is not true. Teachers and schools are engineering certain transitions. I think this concept is very important. It gets us away from the idea of the reception class teacher as one who is just minding the children until they mature, at which point they can be moved on to a teacher who is really going to do some work with them. That is far from the true situation. If we look at the changes made by children in the reception class these transitions seem even more important than those made later in primary school. If teachers monitored these transitions sensitively and individualised their teaching for the slow-to-learn pupils as a result of those observations, they would be improving the quality of their teaching.

The entry class is most important. Where do reception class teachers learn their trade? How much help do they have when they first begin to teach children who are entering school? The more formal the school programme, engineered by the teacher to meet the education system's requirements the more bewildered the new entrant child can become. If the teacher and the system take into account that the child's prior learning has not taught him:

- how to work with a large group of children,
- how to obey institutional rules,
- how to meet the minute by minute expectations of the teacher, and
- how to compete for her attention with many other children,

— in a word, how to interact with this new complex environment so as to profitably learn from it — then the teacher's way of running her room is likely to differ from the procedures which can succeed in higher classes, once children have learned how to act in school. One of my pleas would be that the teacher asked to take a new entrant class be someone with experience of young learners, and that an initial and continuing training period be provided for them as they adapt to the new task. For children this first year at school is a very important time.

In 1964 I watched children's progress through the first year of school by taking records at weekly intervals of what they were doing and what they were saying. To give two examples of the long-term outcomes of their progress, one of the boys who went along fairly slowly for the first six months ended up with marks in the 90's for six subjects in School Certificate (a national examination taken in the third year of secondary school). Another boy at the same school got into a terrible tangle in the first year, had severe reading problems, went to a reading clinic for several years and finally passed School Certificate. That was a success story for a child whose whole schooling has been a trouble to him because of the inappropriate learning that he did in the first year at school. At the end of this study I was saying that we ought to reduce our new entrant classes; we ought not to let them rise above 25 children. Now I would set that goal lower, at a maximum roll of 20 for the first year at school. The purpose of this is to meet each child where he is, arrange instruction so that he can proceed from his strengths and ensure that all children move into schooling without confusions, and with a sense of success.

In New Zealand we have children entering school throughout the year, on their fifth birthdays. We recognise that children will become ready to join the book reading programme at different rates, some within a month or two months of entry to school, the average children not until 5:6 and some children not until the end of the first year.

There is considerable variation in the rate at which New Zealand children move into simple graded material. In my opinion, the explanation for these delays, is not that the child is taking a year to mature but that he is taking a year to learn the early reading behaviours that are the foundation of later success when he is introduced to simple graded texts. The children have these behaviours when they enter school, some take about six months to learn them, some take at least a year. We can pick up some children at six years who have not acquired effective control of these early reading behaviours.

Here I want to add a critical note. We have individualised the rate at which we introduce children to programmes, but I don't believe we have paid sufficient attention to individualising the tasks and instruction that we provide during that period. It is not only that these children are moving at different rates; some of them need more help with some aspects of the task than others.

Observing Progress

To be able to detect these needs we will have to observe a little more closely than we have in the past, what the five-year-old is doing and what he is capable of. Some of my work has been directed towards providing teachers with some structured situations in which they can improve their observation of children's actual behaviour to record with greater accuracy what they can do, and by implication, what they cannot do.

If there is no magical moment at which a child is 'ready' what can we look for in the first year that indicates progress? I look for movement or change in the child's behaviour. My criteria for progress during the first year would be that he moves from those responses he can give when he comes to school toward some other goals that I see as appropriate for him. I am looking for *movement in appropriate directions*. And only careful monitoring will assure me that the child is not practising inappropriate behaviours. For if I do not watch what he is doing, and if I do not capture what is happening in records of some kind, Johnny, who never gets under my feet and who never comes really into a situation where I can truly see what he is doing, may, in fact, for six months or even a year, practise behaviours that will handicap him in reading.

One of the critical areas is directional behaviour. The boy who had some difficulty in getting School Certificate was a boy who was quite confused about direction. At the end of the first year he would happily go from right to left as often as he would go from left to right. Visual learning in reading is nonsense if you don't happen to be looking at the print in the appropriate direction. That is what had happened to him. Organising for preventing reading failure depends a great deal on providing opportunities for observing just what children are doing.

I would like to expand on this idea of observing. My emphasis on this came from my work as a researcher rather than from my work as a teacher. I decided that because the explanations in books did not seem to account for my successes with remedial clients I would pretend that I knew nothing about what reading is and what we should do in reading. I would adopt a neutral stance and observe exactly what children did. In taking this position I stepped out of a teaching role entirely and became much more like a scientist setting up a situation and recording precisely what happens.

When I write of observing children closely this is what I mean! There must be times when the teacher stops teaching and becomes an observer, a time when she must drop all her pre-suppositions about what this child is like, and when she listens very carefully and records very precisely what the child can in fact do.

One must organise for such observation times. In this situation it is difficult not to prompt, to help, to teach, to question. These activities do not have any place in the observation situation which is a completely different thing. To prevent reading failure teachers must have time to observe what children are able to do. This means time out from teaching, time set aside for observing. The younger the child and the poorer the reader, the more time the teacher requires for observing and for thinking about what she observes.

A Check After One Year At School

Knowing the pressures on teachers one has to be realistic about this. What would be the most economical time from the teachers' point of view to carry out thorough observation checks to catch up the children who are either confused or not making progress? I hope the class teacher would observe her children as often as possible, from week to week perhaps. But drastic changes occur in children's lives. Children change school, children change classes, they lose parents who leave the home, they have intermittent absences for legitimate health reasons. It is not sufficient to leave the decision to observe or not, to the class teacher. Towards the end of the first year at school somebody should be responsible for checking on reading behaviour.

Why do I recommend this at the end of the child's first year in New Zealand? It allows the checking process to go on all year, for it would be impossible to carry out this type of check on all children at the one time, say, at the end of a year. The child is given sufficient time to adjust to the school situation. The child who is slow to begin can be given a variety of opportunities to make progress. The teacher who finds that a certain focus within the programme does not suit the child can emphasise a different aspect. The sixth birthday check maximises the opportunities, minimises the pressure on the child, and does not leave the child for more than one year to practise bad habits that might handicap him and be very hard to unlearn. If you leave it until some of the children are 6:6 you have shortened the time for remedial help before the question of Standard One promotion comes up. The longer we leave them, the shorter time we have, and the more they have practised inappropriate responding.

The six-year-old check does call for organising. The ST(JC)* must, in the first instance, be allocated time for this task, to establish the programme in her school, but the ST(JC) can then introduce her staff to the six-year-old checks. We must organise for this sixth birthday check. When we have applied the six-year-old check, obviously, we will need some very skilful teachers to teach children who have been defined by the observation procedures as children with special needs. Inexperienced teachers are little help to slow children, or to children with difficulties who are slow, or to children with difficulties who are

reading their first books. The children with special needs will be hard to teach. The teacher needs experience with a wide variety of approaches, and the ingenuity and flexibility to do different things with different children. Within a school this calls for organising so that you can have these kind of people available for the children sorted out by the six-year-old check.

These skilful teachers should be given recognition for the kind of job they are able to do. The task may not be very rewarding. It is not quite as exciting as taking a high progress group. It is a job that carries more strain, and one's pupils will, inevitably, have lower achievement than those of other teachers at the end of the year. The school has to recognise that this person is a very important person and needs appropriate rewards for tackling this task. The response of these children will not be rapid, even when you give them a highly skilled and experienced teacher, who uses special techniques. Only some of them will make a spurt in that second year and 'catch up'. The children who do this will be the children who have not really taken much notice of the programme in the first year and who now begin to take notice and to learn. In my studies there were only one or two such children. Most children who have made little progress by six years are children who brought some limitation or handicap to school, who are going to carry that handicap with them and who are going to have to learn to read in spite of it.

What can one look for in early reading in order to prevent failure? Let me make an analogy with mathematics and the changes we have seen there in the last few years. Almost nobody now thinking about the young child moving into learning maths is going to think in terms of how many arithmetical items he knows. Almost everybody will be thinking 'what mathematical operations can he carry out'! Although we may not yet have definitive descriptions of the strategies or operations used or to be acquired in early reading this is the kind of shift in our thinking we have to make. In order to prevent early reading failure *we should be looking for strategies the child is using*. We have to observe him reading book material as well as checking on his word recognition. You can hear a child correcting himself as he reads. As he is reading along, he stops, he goes back. Nobody suggested that he should do this. This is a strategy that tells me he is monitoring his own reading. If he is listening to what he is saying he has recognised that something doesn't fit, goes back, and he takes responsibility for working on it.

This does relate to organising for reading. The high progress readers move into reading, they get certain help and then by the time they are about six years of age, they are monitoring their own reading in helpful ways. If they are given material of an appropriate level they have some strategies which will help them to teach themselves from that material.

The child who is not able to do this monitoring of his

*Senior or supervising teacher for Junior classes

own reading is the one who needs the teacher. Observation records of teachers show that they allow good readers to read much more than they do slow readers. There are reasons why this occurs. The slow child takes longer to read, and he is reading much more limited text. The high progress reader is reading involved text and takes several pages to get through an important part of the story. If there is anything in this about organising, it suggests that if we simply manipulate twice as much time for the slow children as for the good readers we might in fact be doing quite a lot for the prevention of reading failure.

So it is important to look for strategies, to look for progress in the child's reading strategies, and particularly to see that children are getting to the point where they in fact can tutor themselves. Situations must be set up where they can carry on without much attention from the teacher. This leaves her more time to work with slow progress readers.

Advantages of Individual Instruction

A major problem in thinking about what school organisation will improve the quality of instruction, is the individual learner versus the group instruction dilemma. Formal education procedures are, of necessity, group procedures, but the best progress for a particular child will result from individual instruction. Our compromise between the large class procedure and the individual one is to group children. This is our dilemma. How do we meet individual learning needs even under group instruction procedures? One cannot justify teaching all children on the assumption that all need the same kind of teaching. Teachers do recognise the great differences between children, and within children, and in their background experiences and personality traits.

The need for organising reading instruction in order to provide in an adequate way for individual differences is recognised but much still remains to be done in practical application. This implies different programmes for different children, not just different rates.

There is a strong emphasis on individual tuition in the present system in Sweden. One of the main regulations of the Swedish Education Acts of 1962 and 1969 is that the personal resources of the individual child must not only be respected but must be the starting point for the planning of education and teaching. According to objectives stated in the school law the school must stimulate the child's personal growth towards his development as a free, self-active, self-confident, harmonious human being. The school *must* give individual education.

Some steps taken in Sweden to further a diagnostic approach and the individualisation of the teaching of reading are these:

• Class size has been reduced to a maximum of 25 in the first three years — but the average size for the country as a whole for the first three years lies between 17 and 18 children per class.
• Better opportunities than before are provided for individual tutoring, small group teaching, teaching in clinics and the provision of special classes of various kinds.
• In the first three grades, there is now written into the teaching load of each teacher, a weekly two-hour block of time for tutoring any individual child in her class who, in her judgment, needs such help. Obviously there has to be organisation for this when it is part of the teacher's weekly work.
• Another procedure has contributed significantly to the individualisation of teaching. In the first grade, for example, one half of the class meets with the teacher for the first two hours of the day. The second half comes to school two hours late and stays two hours later on. This kind of staggering might be organised for if there was extra help around. This is an interesting way to reduce numbers and getting more individual instruction for children having particular difficulties.

To prevent reading disabilities, observation of children's progress, and individual teaching for some children are recommended.

In summary

To help those children who are becoming reading cripples in the first year of schooling, we do have to organise:

• For using strengths of teaching staffs at appropriate points.
• For new teaching staff to have opportunities to gain these strengths by observing people who are expert in working with them.
• For opportunities to see precisely where a child is, what strategies he is employing.
• For picking up those children who are employing strategies which are going to be an impediment to their progress.
• To give more reading time to those children who are making slow progress.
• For individual teaching.

There will always be a challenge in meeting individual differences when children enter school because at that time children are very different in so many ways. Teachers must be observant of individuals' responses and of individual progress. They must be aware of the alternate learning sequences which can lead to progress, and they must know when progress is not occurring. Organising effectively for meeting individual needs in the first year of school is important, *especially* for children who are slow to move into the programme.

6 Reducing Reading Difficulties With a Second Chance to Learn

Whatever the origins of reading difficulties they have a large learned component. They limit achievement in school learning. They get worse if untreated and many pupils get further behind their classmates over time even when they receive available treatments. Surprisingly, although what is difficult about reading differs markedly from child to child the programmes they have been placed in have often been prescriptive and general.

If the young school entrant has not been able to learn in the classroom programme after one year at school, what happens if the education system organises to provide him with individual instruction each day in a programme which starts with what he can do and takes him along his own particular route into reading and writing? At the organisational level that is what the Reading Recovery programme does. Research (see p. 84) has shown that a large percentage of children who were the poorest readers in their schools after one year at school responded quickly to such an approach. Resources saved by the rapid progress of these children to average levels of performance can be directed to the very small percentage who need help for a longer term.

Reading Recovery is based on two assumptions. The first is that a programme for a child having difficulty learning to read should be based on a detailed observation of that child as a reader and writer, with particular attention to what that child can do. The programme will work out of these strengths and not waste time teaching anything already known. The second assumption is that we need to know how children who become readers learn to read so that children who are having difficulty can be helped along that same path. The progressions will vary slightly from one education system to another.

My observations of successful children reading led to my view of reading acquisition expressed in *Reading: The Patterning of Complex Behaviour* (1979). The observation procedures outlined in the first part of this book provide a basis for describing what a particular child has learned about reading and writing. What else is required for a second chance programme?

Individual Instruction

The gains recorded for the Reading Recovery programme have been made with individual instruction. It sounds like an expensive approach but has proved to be economical for two reasons. Many children move through the programme very quickly, in an average of 13-14 weeks and their places are then taken by other children. Then, after leaving the programme the children have been able to move forward with average children in their classes and very few have needed further help.

It makes a great deal of sense to change our teaching approach for children who are not making progress after one year of the classroom programme, and to give them individual lessons which work from the child's responses not from the teacher's programme.

The child who does not know when his attempts are good and when they are poor is reinforced by the teacher immediately he makes an appropriate response. The teacher's close supervision will also allow her to detect an interferring or handicapping type of response when it creeps in, and to swiftly arrange for a better response to occur. She may structure the task (for example, provide a masking card or a pointer) or she may note the need to teach some new basis for making choices between words.

The result of individual programming is that programmes differ from child to child. One teacher per pupil is the only practical way of working with children who have extreme difficulty in learning to read.

Acceleration

The child requiring help with reading has been making very slow progress and has been dropping further and further behind his classmates. If he were to become an average progress child he would have to make fast progress, faster than his classmates, in order to catch up to them. Acceleration refers to this rate of progress.

To say that the slow progress child who cannot be pushed or placed under stress should now learn at an accelerated rate seems to be a puzzling contradiction. However, I have already discussed two important factors which help this to occur. He will get one-to-one teaching and the programme will start with his strengths and proceed according to his needs.

In addition, whenever possible the child will read and write text. He will not be diverted from printed texts to pictorial material or puzzles but will be taught what he needs to learn in the context of continuous text. (There might be good reasons for a rare exception to this.) The learning of detail such as the sounds of letters or a list of words is completed through text reading and text writing, and his interactions with his teacher.

Acceleration depends upon teacher selection of the clearest, easiest, most memorable examples with which to establish a new response, skill, principle or procedure. For example the child, trying to recall how to use a prefix, may be helped by the first example of a prefix that he learned. The teacher needs to select examples which are very productive. Productive examples lead to further reading control in a number of different ways.

It is not enough with problem readers for the teacher to have rapport, to generate interesting tasks and generally to be a good teacher. The teacher must be able to design a superbly sequenced programme determined by the child's performance, and to make highly skilled decisions moment by moment during the lesson.

The child must never engage in unnecessary activities because that wastes learning time. If the teacher judges that a child can make a small leap forward, she must watch the effects of this decision and take immediate supportive action if necessary. An expert teacher will help the child to leap appropriately rather than walk the child through her programme step by step.

Acceleration is achieved as the child takes over the learning process and works independently, discovering new things for himself, inside and outside the lessons. He comes to push the boundaries of his own knowledge.

The principle of acceleration is not an easy one to implement and must be constantly borne in mind. During our training a teacher is challenged if she seems to be wasting the learner's time, especially when her peers notice that she is teaching something the child has already shown that he could do!

Two kinds of learning must be kept in balance: on the one hand there is fluency and performing with success on familiar material and on the other there is a challenge to independent problem-solving on new and interesting texts with supportive teaching. The texts are very carefully selected for the needs of a particular pupil to foster acceleration.

Daily Instruction, Intensive Programme

Reading Recovery lessons are given daily. In that way even the child who cannot remember from day to day can be helped. The teacher acts as the memory of what his response was yesterday, and prompts him accordingly. (Twice a week lessons are a weak approach to meeting special learning needs. Twice a week with a group of children *makes it impossible* to design the programme to meet the needs of the individual learner.)

The principles of an intensive programme allow the close supervision of the shifts in the child's responding. Short lessons held often are important for success.

Getting Down to Detail

In learning to read the child making normal progress picks up and organises for himself a wealth of detailed information about letters, print, words and reading with a spontaneity that leads teachers to believe that many things do not have to be taught. There is evidence that this attention to print in the environment, in books, and in early attempts to write begins early in the preschool years for some children. Others, however, may have given it little thought.

From time to time the child having difficulty in learning to read may have to pay attention to the detail of print. Letter learning must be done, *although it is not necessary to postpone book reading until letters are known*. There will be a gradual accumulation of letter knowledge as the child reads and writes. Some children will need particular attention to letter formation, not 'to get it right' from the point of view of good writing but because these few children cannot analyse the form into its parts, or cannot find a learned routine for producing it.

When the teacher becomes involved in teaching for detail the prospect of acceleration is seriously threatened. The child cannot afford to spend much time practising detail, and he may become addicted to it and find it difficult later to take a wider approach to the reading act. Tuition on detail may aim to fill a small gap, or to clear a confusion. It should be a detour from a programme whose main focus is reading books. The detour may be taken to pay attention to some particular aspect of print in the clear realisation that knowledge of the detail is of very limited value on its own. It must in the end be used in the service of reading continuous text. Details must receive attention but always in a subsidiary status to message getting.

Sequence

Every school and classroom has some teaching sequence by which reading is presented to children. For the child who has become a reading failure in that setting it will probably not be sufficient to change to a different teacher, different material and a different approach to instruction.

This remedy is often suggested, but I have not found it sufficient. Failing children differ more among themselves in response to curriculum than average children. They are a heterogeneous group whose strengths and weaknesses are different and whose learning tangles may need quite different programme details to untangle them. Programmes and teaching sequences of any standard kind are unlikely to meet the needs of severely retarded readers. While a commercial kit may be a slight improvement on nothing, the ideal programme will have activities individually selected to meet the needs of a particular child.

It therefore rests with the teacher to know the way in which reading skill develops, the teaching sequences that are possible and the short-cuts that are permissible. To be able to pick and choose among teaching techniques and learning activities, the teacher must be very familiar with her subject. An experienced teacher is the best remedial teacher because she has an inner awareness of sequence in the programme around which she can vary the particular lessons.

Most school programmes will have established a series of books as the gradient of difficulty through which their children progress, and they refer to children's progress levels in terms of such books. Other programmes may leave children free to read story books, graded roughly for difficulty and will assess progress by some other means, such as a standardised text, or an informal prose inventory on a graded set of text material.

A Reading Recovery teacher wishing to bring her students to the levels of achievement of their average classmates will need to have some sequence of difficulty through which she attempts to move her students. Our programme used many different books but an attempt is made to grade these simple story books against some benchmark series. A book may be selected because it can contribute to a particular child's learning problem of the moment but the teacher knows the level at which that book can be equated to the benchmark series. The instruction needs to be related to the progressions in the reading series used in the school or the classroom programme, but it need not take place on that series of books. Teachers can keep a child for weeks on one level, choosing books of parallel difficulty until the child is ready for the next step. On the other hand the teacher may help the child to jump forward three steps, support his initial uncertainty and be able to conclude that the acceleration was justified. In both these cases the child would not usually be reading the graded material of the classroom series but material known to be of equivalent difficulty (see p. 2).

Reciprocal Gains of Reading and Writing

The child who has failed to learn to read is often also retarded in writing stories. Often remedial lessons exclude the teaching of writing as this is seen as some extension that comes after reading or a different subject. An alternative view sees reading and writing in the early acquisition stage as both contributing to learning about print. (They are separated by educators for timetables and curricula.) A case can be made for the theory that learning to write letters, words and sentences actually helps the child to make the visual discriminations of detail in print that he will use in his reading (Clay, 1982).

Children write stories every day. It is in the writing part of the daily lesson that children are required to pay attention to letter detail, letter order, sound sequences, and letter sequences, and the links between messages in oral language and messages in printed language. The writing knowledge serves as a resource of information that can help the reader and vice versa. The child comes to control a high frequency vocabulary for writing and learns strategies for spelling more and more words in his language. Reading and writing are interwoven throughout the programme and teaching proceeds on the assumption that both provide cues and responses which facilitate new responding in either area.

Reading knowledge tends to draw ahead of writing knowledge after a while but at the beginning of school what the child can write is a good indicator of what the child knows in detail about written language.

7 The Shape of the Reading Recovery Child's Programme

Do you know how reading is taught in your school? Do you know what reading processes are being trained in those children who succeed? You ought to. It is important information for anyone to have if they are to try to make judgements about the reading problems of the other pupils in the same school. Any reading programme has its 'risk areas', in that it stresses some facets of the reading process and must as a consequence give less attention to other aspects.

Early intervention calls for sensitive observation of the children making slow progress:

- in the context of the sequences of skill acquisition observed in the children making satisfactory progress,
- in the light of clear descriptions of the teaching, the day-to-day activities, and the sequential progressions of the programme.

I do not need an elaborate definition of reading difficulties. One simply takes the pupil — child, adolescent or adult — from where he is, to somewhere else. There is not one of us who could not read better if we had individual instruction in reading now.

Two assumptions are made in the outline that follows. The first is that a classroom programme will continue alongside the extra tuition. And the second is that the extra tutoring will be individual.

Roaming Around The Known

For the first two weeks of the tutoring programme stay with what the child already knows. Do not introduce *any* new learning. The Diagnostic Survey will have shown up some of the things that the child can do. During the first two weeks watch for and record other behaviours that you notice.

Go over what he knows in different ways until your ingenuity runs out, and until he is moving fluently around this personal corpus of responses, the letters, words and messages that he knows how to read or write.

There are several reasons why this period of roaming around the known makes a good starting point for the child's Reading Recovery programme.

- The observation techniques are only sampling procedures and this period gives the teacher a further opportunity to observe more of the child's ways of responding.

- The child and the teacher have an opportunity to get to know each other.
- The teacher is free to observe the child without the need to record all that occurs or think particularly of programme implications.
- The teacher works with reading texts and writing texts (and not with letters or words). This seems to give the child a feeling that he is 'really reading'.
- The child may discover responses that he did not think he knew and in an unpressured situation he may observe new relationships.
- At the end of the period the child will feel comfortable with a small body of knowledge, confident enough to use this as a springboard for trying new things when the programme starts. This is a firm foundation on which the teacher can build.

However, the most important reasons for roaming around the known is that it requires the teacher to stop teaching from her preconceived ideas. She has to work from the child's responses. This will be her focus throughout the programme.

Find a readable text

Find some kind of text material that the child can read at about 90% accuracy or better. Don't guess. Measure it by taking a running record, even if it is only a couple of lines of print. In your search for a simple text which the child can read the following provide a list of texts which get easier as you go down it:

- an easy book
- a simple book about the child's own experiences
- a very simple story you have read to this pupil
- a simple story that you write for this pupil keeping to his known vocabulary
- a simple text he has dictated.

Each of these is moving one step closer to the child's limited horizons. The better he is the further up the sequence you can start. The poorer he is the lower down that sequence you should start. You cannot rely on a published sequence of material for these earliest lessons. *The teacher must be the expert chooser and sequencer of the texts for a Reading Recovery pupil. This is critical.*

Think about this child's responses

Use the first two weeks of lessons to find out how he responds in a teaching relationship. Make yourself specify just how he responds. Put it into words. What does he do well? What strategies does he try? How does he help himself? What more have you noticed about the letters, words and other features of print that he knows?

Encourage writing

Add to the information from the Diagnostic Survey by finding out more about what he can write, out of his head. Record what he can do. At all times keep records of what you discover that he can do.

Build fluency on the very little he knows

Hold his interest, bolster his confidence, make him your co-worker. Get the responding fluent and habituated but even at this stage encourage flexibility, using the same knowledge in different ways. Confidence, ease, flexibility and, with luck, discovery are the keynotes of this period which I have called 'roaming around the known'. Do not move too soon; be sure the foundation is firm and the child confident. Both the child and the teacher should be straining at the leash and wanting to go further, but resist the temptation. Most children need this two week period before new material is introduced.

New behaviours may appear

Now you will probably notice some things emerging that you did not think the child knew. New and useful behaviours appear as he begins to relate things one to another. He remembers a book with this or that in it. A letter reminds him of his uncle's name. He reads *car* for *are* or some such mismatch that makes you feel he is getting closer to effective decisions about uncertainty.

There are two reasons for this appearance of new behaviours. The child has many strategies which he uses to solve problems in his daily life. He is now beginning to apply these to reading. Why didn't he do this before? When one is having difficulty with a task one tries several approaches. As each fails one ceases to try them. The failing reader has stopped using many strategies because he could not make them work. If you pitch the text at an easy level, and you support him in using the things he can do you will find that he begins to try again some of these discarded strategies. You should show delight at this spontaneous relating of 'this to that'.

So you unleash those discarded approaches this child has ceased to use on the text. You probably will not achieve this if you have pre-determined your programme or are using some author's published programme. But you will have more luck if you are responding to the child in an individual instruction situation. It only works well if the individual child's capacities determine the programme.

Moving Into Instruction

A typical tutoring session

In Reading Recovery a typical tutoring session would include each of these activites, usually in the following order, as the format of the daily lesson.

- re-reading of two or more familiar books — *text*
- re-reading yesterday's new book and taking a running record — *text*
- letter identification (plastic letters on a magnetic board) — *letters*
- writing a story (including hearing sounds in words) — *text* — *sounds*
- cut-up story to be rearranged — *text*
- new book introduced — *text*
- new book attempted — *text*

There are several reasons for placing the new book at the end of the lesson, although some teachers have argued that the child is tired by this stage. Individual variations in lesson plans are always possible, providing there is a sound rationale based on a particular child's response to lessons.

The main reason for placing the new book at the end of the lesson is that each previous activity has encouraged the child to work on his own problems and to actively engage in problem-solving. By the end of the lesson he should have revised easy reading, letter knowledge, links between letters and sounds, his monitoring strategies in the cut-up story, and he should tackle his new book with his repertoire of responses in their most accessible form.

The second reason is that any new learning required for the new book can be introduced and practised during the other segments of the lesson.

The third reason for this placement of the new book is that there will be a minimum of interference between this timing and the re-reading of the book the next day.

Introducing new material

At this early stage there are some useful do's and don'ts which help to keep the task easy.

- Make sure the child can hear a distinction or difference between two sounds or two words before you teach him to *see* the difference.
- Start with large units not the smallest ones
— separate words out of phrases
— separate letters out of words.
- Encourage the use of hand and eye together. The use of the eyes alone comes later in the learning sequence.
- Link something the child does easily with something he finds hard (for support) before asking for the difficult response on its own.

- Teach by demonstration. Use a questioning approach only for established responses.
- Aim to teach a few *items* (letters, words, sounds) and then try to establish further examples by *strategies of comparison*. Teaching all the items in a category is a teacher's hang-up. What the child needs to know is a few items and some strategies for picking up new ones later, as he reads.

Confusions

Now turn to the child's confusions. Without increasing the difficulty level and keeping to text reading, record and think about this particular child's confusions. Plan an attack on them. Talk to another couple of teachers about the easiest way to go from where he is to less confusion. That way you will find out what a blinkered approach each of us has to these difficulties and to teaching sequences. Probably you and your colleagues will not agree. Never mind. You have added their hypotheses to your own and can now approach the child's confusions tentatively, and with an open mind. With reading recovery cases do not rely on your own hunches. Be objective and critical of your own assumptions.

Some pointers about confusions are:

- Don't present them side by side. Get Item A well established and known for several weeks before you bring back Item B.
- Don't teach by the least noticeable difference principle. That is not the way we play 'Twenty Questions'.
- Is the child's difficulty in *seeing* a difference? If so, have him dictate, write, cut up and reassemble texts.
- Is the child's difficulty in *hearing* a difference? If so, articulate for him and with him very slowly, and teach him to use this strategy himself.
- Is the child's difficulty with order or sequence? If so, get him to dictate, read, cut up and reassemble and write a simple text.

You will probably have to move away from texts and into detail at this point. Resolve that this is a *temporary but necessary detour*, and plan to get back to text reading as soon as possible, preferably within the same lesson.

Developing a self-improving system

Plan to encourage a self-improving system and reinforce this.

- Give the child ways to detect error for himself.
- Encourage attempts to correct error.
- Give him clues to aid self-correction.
- Allow him to make checks or repetitions so he can confirm his first attempts.
- When he works out a word or text for himself, help him to know how he did it. Ask him 'How did you know?' (See page 74.)

Increasing text difficulty

Cautiously increase the text difficulty and repeat the sequence. Give massive practice on texts at this next level before you increase the difficulty level again.

Now look at what he cannot do

Offer him many things. Pay particular attention to what you think would have the greatest payoff. This might be:

- an intensive vocabulary spree
- a training in predicting what structures come next
- a training in hearing sound sequences, first and last sounds and clusters of sounds
- a shift from sounding to syllabic attack
- letter identification.

Get those two colleagues together again and listen to their ideas on priorities and the way to achieve them. That exposes your assumptions to critical analysis. Keep the principles used in the games 'Twenty Questions' or 'Animal, Vegetable or Mineral', in mind.

Now go back to your pupil and ask him what he would like to learn next and try to work this in with your priorities.

Some organisational points

Keep all those processes going *but* arrange for massive opportunity to read enchantingly interesting texts of just the right difficulty, over a longer period than anyone anticipated — and after the child and parents and class teacher want you to stop.

Developing effective strategies

Reading Recovery procedures have sometimes been questioned because they appear to require correct responding from children. This is not true.

There is a particular opportunity for revision and reworking in the one-to-one teaching situation. Child and teacher are talking about the reading or the writing as it occurs. There is opportunity for the child to initiate dialogue about his response as he works and for the teacher to help in many different ways. However, the programme sets the highest value on independent responding, and this must involve risks of being wrong. What the teacher will do is set some priorities as to which kinds of new learning she will attend to — just one or two things — and let the other behaviours that were incorrect go unattended at this time.

The goal of the teaching is to assist the child to produce effective strategies for working on text, not to accumulate items of knowledge. It is necessary to develop self-correction by allowing room for self-correction to be initiated by the child. A teacher who demanded correct responding would not be developing self-correcting behaviours!

Any theoretical position which includes self-monitoring and self-correcting as significant behaviour in reading or in writing implies the existence of near misses, uncorrected responses and sometimes corrected responses. The important thing about the self-corrections is that the child initiates them because the child sees that something is wrong and calls up his own resources for working on a solution.

An example of reading book progress

Rochelle had almost a full programme of tutoring but may have been discontinued at too low a level. She made steady progress in the following year but three years later her progress was slower than average. She had 17 weeks in tutoring and only 41 lessons (obviously not a daily programme). She entered the programme at Red 1 level (New Zealand Ready to Read books) and at that time was just beginning to recognise words in text. Rochelle read 22 little books before she began her climb up through the reading levels. At each level she read several story books. Her teacher usually recorded her accuracy on the 'benchmark' books, the Ready to Read books, and those are what are recorded on the table. The teacher's choice of books and her timing of the increase in difficulty level shows excellent judgement and good pacing of her pupil.

Rochelle's pattern of progress should not be taken as a model. Each child's selection of books, rate of progress, starting and finishing points will be different. All that Rochelle's record shows is how the shape of a Reading Recovery programme worked out for one child.

Books Read, Book Level and Difficulty Level for the Child: Rochelle				
Week of Programme	Title		Difficult* for the child	Equivalent Ready To Read Book Level**
1-4	(22 Titles)[1]		(No accuracy records)	
5	Cuckoo In The Nest	(PM)	Easy	3
5	Merry-Go-Round (plus 1 title)	(PM)	Easy	3
7	The Fire Engine (plus 1 title)	(R-to-R)	Easy	5
7	Planes (plus 1 title)	(PM)	Easy	5
8	The Escalator	(Star)	Easy	6
8	Going To School	(R-to-R)	Instructional	7
10	Playtime	(R-to-R)	Easy	8
10	Christmas Shopping (plus 1 title)	(R-to-R)	Easy	9
10	Saturday Morning (plus 2 titles)	(R-to-R)	Easy	10
11	The Christmas Tree (plus 1 title)	(PM)	Easy	11
11	Painting The Shed	(R-to-R)	Easy	11
12	A Country School (plus 1 title)	(R-to-R)	Easy	12
13	The Pet Show (plus 1 title)	(R-to-R)	Easy	13
14	At The Camp (plus 1 title)	(R-to-R)	—	—
16	A Wet Morning (plus 1 title)	(PM)	Instructional	14
16	The Little Red Bus	(PM)	Instructional	13
16	The Pets Run Away (plus 4 titles)	(Playtime)	Instructional	14

*   Easy 95-100% accuracy achieved   /   Instructional 90-94% accuracy achieved   /   Hard below 90% accuracy.

** Equated to the graded series, Ready To Read. This is a post hoc rating. The wide range of supplementary and story books used were not graded for equivalence to levels in the Ready To Read series until 1980 (Watson, 1980).

[1] This refers to other books read but not named here.

8 Reading Recovery Teaching Procedures

These teaching procedures were developed with children who had been at school for one year and who were unable to make satisfactory progress in their classrooms. It is unnecessary to teach most children in these ways.

The procedures are arranged so that a teacher can turn to the approach she requires for a particular child with a particular problem. Many of the suggestions that are detailed will not be appropriate for some children. As these procedures were being developed over a three year period we became convinced that the difficulties which children have in learning to read differ markedly from child to child (see Reading Recovery Research Reports page 84). *The teacher must skilfully select the activities needed by a particular child.* Otherwise she will retard the child further by having him complete unnecessary work thereby wasting precious learning time.

1 Learning About Direction

Introduction

In my studies I have found that learning about direction can be very confusing for young children. Some directional confusions may be found in all beginning readers who are learning the arbitrary rules we use to write down languages. Such confusions persist for some children who are having difficulty in learning to read (see p.20).

Children who have poor motor co-ordination, and those who are quick and impulsive, and those who are timid and do not like to try a new task, may experience directional problems and will require more time than usual and sensitive teaching to establish directional behaviour. Another small group of children who need help are those who have learned and practised peculiar directional habits for a long time.

Recording procedures

Directional behaviour is quite complex when it does not follow the rules of written language. A set of simple procedures for recording it are outlined. They have helped teachers to record what children actually do when they are just learning about direction and print.

Record the child's directional responses to the print in a book with simple text. Ask the child to 'Read it with your finger'. Record any lapse from correct responding.

- Show the horizontal direction with arrows ⟶ ⟶
- Show the vertical direction by numbering the lines

    (3) ⟶
    (2) ⟶
    (1) ⟶

- Show whether the page was a left or right one Lp/Rp.
- Show whether the child used a left or right hand Lh/Rh.

A sample record might look like this:

Page 1 ⟶ $\frac{Lp}{Lh}$ This would mean

Correct direction on a left page pointing with the left hand.

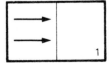

Page 2 ⟶ $\frac{Rp}{Rh}$ On a right page with the right hand the child moved from right-to-left and back on the next line from left-to-right.

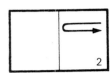

Page 3 ⟵ $\frac{(2)\ Rp}{(1)\ Rh}$ On a right page with the right hand the child moved from right-to-left and from bottom to top.

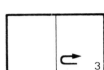

Page 4 ⟵ $\frac{Lp}{Lh}$ On a left page with the left hand the child moved from right-to-left and from left-to-right.

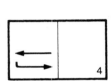

The (tentative) interpretation of this record might be:

- that the child had learned very little about the directional rules of print.
- that he used his left hand on a left page and his right hand on a right page.
- that a starting position at the top left of a page had not been established.
- that top to bottom direction was not consistent.

Recovery procedures

The teacher must give clear demonstrations with few words. She must give praise and positive reinforcement for any attempts that are close to what is required.

Starting position

Check each new book introduced to the child to see that the starting position on a page will not confuse this particular child.

- Accept either hand, whichever he chooses to use.
- Control the directional behaviour by pointing to the starting position on the page or line.
- Provide opportunities for overlearning, i.e. practice well beyond the point where you think the behaviour is learned.
- Prevent the child from starting in the wrong place by various devices, such as intercepting a false move and gently bringing the child's hand to the correct position.

Starting signal
Where the child moves incorrectly across print a signal such as a green sticker (Green light for Go) can be used to indicate the starting point to the left of the text.

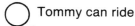 Tommy can ride

The child's working space may need this signal also. So be prepared to use it:

- on the blackboard
- on the table top
- on paper.

Some teachers are surprised when they find that a child who controls direction in one place uses different directional responses in another place.

To assist orientation on more complex text a coloured line or margin can be placed on the left side of the page.

| Tommy can ride
| on his tricycle
| down the road.

A helping hand
Teachers should not be afraid to encourage hand action to assist reading.

For the most difficult cases, passively move the child's hand and arm through the appropriate movements until he can manage without this guidance.

The child's hand will guide his directional behaviour as it becomes more stable in:

- establishing a top-left starting point
- consistent left to right movement across lines
- matching words in speech to words in text, one after the other
- locating the first letter of lines
- locating the first letter of words.

Do away with signals
The child should do away with signals like dots and lines as soon as he has gained some control over the top-left starting position.

Retain hand support for longer
As correct responding becomes more reliable the teacher can begin to require phrasing and fluency. When this is stressed the child will drop the finger-pointing (with encouragement to do this if necessary). He will regress to using hand support:

- when a text is new and difficult
- when he is tired
- when the layout is unusual
- when he is incorporating some new aspect of behaviour into his established system of reading behaviour.

Choice of texts
In the early stages of learning about direction the child will be helped by the use of texts in which the layout is similar and the text begins towards the top-left of the page. As the child gains control over direction more variable layout should be introduced to ensure that he becomes flexible in his approach to print. Aim for stable control over direction before you push for flexibility.

Goal
The goal is a particular movement pattern suited to books, blackboards, paper and all print. It has probably been achieved when the child:

- uses either hand to point to print
- on either page
- without lapse in direction
- or with self-correction following a lapse.

Talk about direction
As an intermediate step it may be necessary for the child to guide his own movement with words that remind him of what to do. This must be unlearned later because the movement pattern must become a habit that is used automatically without requiring the child to attend to it.

So, avoid talking about these action patterns if possible. Model the action for the child as often as he needs this help.

2 Locating Responses

Introduction
Young children have difficulty pointing to a row of objects in sequence one after the other. This has been accepted as important in early mathematics lessons but few have noted that this is also a limitation for reading. It may mean that the child cannot attend to one printed word at a time in sequential order.

Most school entrants can do this or will quickly learn to do this in the first year at school. A few children having difficulty with learning to read will need special help in learning these responses.

Ask a child to point to each word in a simple one line text. If he fails to do this there may be several reasons. Only one reason is considered here; he cannot *attend to, focus on* or *point to* one word after the other.

Use some exercises like those that follow to establish these behaviours.

Recovery procedures
Early learning
One after the other put down two objects in a row. Call

the child's attention to them and point to them one after the other, the left one first. *Don't count them.*

Ask the child to *point* to a row of three objects; four objects; five objects or more; in sequence one after the other. Record:

- the starting point
- the direction
- any difficulties.

Intermediate steps
Repeat the exercise with objects and sequences like felt dots, geometric shapes, pencil dots, two letter words (same and different) five word sentences. *It is probably wise to avoid using single letters.* Record:

- the starting point
- the direction
- any difficulties.

Provide practice, using the appropriate directional pattern for print.

The goal is coordinated, one-to-one correspondence with the movement pattern needed for print and pointing to individual symbols in a set.

Now ask the child to tell you about the objects in sequence. Without pointing:

- name the objects
- name the colour of the dots
- give the number of dots.

Advanced learning
Words and spaces on books with:

- one line per page
- two lines per page
- more than two lines.

If the child needs help to *see* the words and spaces between words write out a line or two of the text of the book in large print exaggerating the spaces.

Cut the sentence up into single words as the child watches. Get the child to remake the sentence and reread it several times, pointing carefully.

You can rearrange the cut-out words with *over-emphasised spaces at first*, gradually reducing these to normal spacing. To develop an accurate locating response on book texts for the child who still has difficulties:

- Use two-finger framing (with two index fingers).
- Use a long pointer. (It requires more effort to control the movement.)
- Encourage deliberate voice pointing.

The extra control needed to accomplish these more difficult motor tasks slows down speech so that the child feels the pauses between the spoken words while his fingers show the boundaries of the written words.

Work for flexibility
Once a good locating response has been established on a familiar book with two-finger framing get the child to read with one-finger pointing.

If you are using cut-up stories — the child's stories that are written out and cut up — these can be rearranged by the teacher in several ways — one line, two lines, three lines, to foster this flexibility:

- I went to the zoo.
- I went
  to the zoo.
- I went
  to the
  zoo.

Take the opportunity to ask the child to read a few words of the story on each rearrangement.

As a more advanced task cut-up stories can be rearranged *by the child*. The teacher alters the size of the space in which the child is asked to remake the story.

- Making it larger I   am   a   big   girl
- Making it progressively smaller I am a
                                   big girl

The children who have most difficulty with learning about direction tend to have problems with this type of task.

Too many breaks
Over-segmenting can cause difficulties with one to one correspondence. For example:

A	way	we	go
Away	we	go	to

To overcome a bad case of too many breaks exaggerate the segments with magnetic letters spatially and also with shouting or singing, then gradually rejoin the two segments again.

A — way
Away

Caution. For most children the activities described in this section will be unnecessary. They learn these things incidentally while exploring books in a more enjoyable way.

There is no point in delaying a child's progress with such a detailed programme unless these activities have value for a particular problem that has not responded to other approaches.

3 Spatial Layout

Introduction

In trying to write stories some children have become very confused about how to use the space on the page. Perhaps this stems from their confused concepts of the relationships of letters to words. If the child shows confusion these activities may help.

Recovery procedures

With letters and words

• In word study use *magnetic letters* to overlearn the positioning of letters in making a word. Exaggerate the space between letters in some well known words and get the child to return them to the normal spacing.
• Use *magnetic letters* to accentuate the spaces between words and get the child to return them to normal spacing.

In writing

• *In writing* help the child to leave a finger space between words, saying 'It is easier for us to read'.
• Give the child help to use the space on the page in spacing his sentences. This help might mean giving a definite starting position — top left hand corner.

In cut-up stories

• *In cut-up stories* help the child to remake the story several times, each time altering the space in which he is working so that he is forced to reorganise the layout of the story to fit the 'spatial frame' which you have created by your use of the table top.

The aim in these activities is to give the child the ability to organise himself in relation to written language space. Therefore any aids and props should be used only for the period for which they are essential.

An important note

We have not found lined paper a help for story writing. It seems to impose too many constraints on the child who has difficulty with spatial learning or with confusions. But cues and prompts as aids on the blank unlined paper work well.

4 Writing stories

Introduction

Many of the operations needed in early reading are practised in another form in early writing.

This is not a matter of copying words and stories: it concerns going from ideas to spoken words to printed messages.

First lessons in a reading recovery programme will have explored what letters and words the child can write. From a very few these should be expanded as quickly as letter learning will allow.

Elkonin analysis and word building with magnetic letters are also supportive activities for early writing.

These should be concurrent activities. They need not precede the introduction of child-dictated stories (see Clay, 1975).

The focus of these procedures is on getting the child to produce his own written stories.

Recovery procedures

For these stories reading recovery teachers used unlined exercise books, turned sideways. The child drew the picture and wrote his story on the page nearest him. His attempts to write words, teacher-written models or boxes for hearing sounds in sequence were all placed on the top page.

```
┌─────────────────────┐
│                     │
│  Working space for  │
│  teaching and trials│
│                     │
├─────────────────────┤
│                     │
│      Child's        │
│      story          │
│                     │
└─────────────────────┘
```

Child dictates a story

The child is invited to tell a story (sentence) about the previous book read or about the best part of the story, or about some topic of interest to him.

Talk with the child about:

• something he has done
• a story he has heard or read
• a TV programme he has seen
• something that interests him
• an experience you have had together.

Suggest that he draws a picture about it. Provide felt pens, coloured pencils, ballpoint pens for him to choose from. (This activity will gradually take up less time as writing confidence grows. Before long the picture must be omitted.)

Encourage him to tell you a story (sentence) about it. Repeat the child's story. Scribble down the sentence for your own reference.

Sometimes you may want to help the child to word the sentence so that it contains words he can write, but do this very rarely.

Child writes
Encourage the child to write as much as he can alone each session. Encourage him to write the words you think he might know. Praise him for his efforts. The child may write the words he thinks he knows on his practice page first, if he needs to check on himself. The teacher may write some of the easier words on the practice page for him to copy or write the difficult words into the story for him.

Get fluency
When the child writes a word you want him to know next time say, '*Do it again. And again. Now write it here. And here. Do it faster. Once more.*'
This procedure helps the child to practise producing the *sequence* of letters needed for that word.

- It builds fluency.
- It helps the child to remember the word in every detail.

Come back to this word again next day, or for several days asking each time for the same fluent writing.

Take a minute at the beginning or end of a lesson to review the most recent words you have taken to fluency, providing help if necessary.

Try to get flexibility as well as fluency by having the child construct the word with chalk, with magnetic letters, with his finger on the desk, or water on a board, on a wipe-out board or an acetate sheet with felt pen.

Later
- When he comes to a problem word help him to attend to and isolate at least the initial sound and to predict what he would expect to see at the beginning. Then write the word for him to copy.
- Use sound sequence analysis techniques described in the next section (Section 5).

Errors in stories
One way to approach this problem is to anticipate a child's difficulty or offer help before errors occur. Another approach is to allow the child to stop when he recognises that something has gone wrong, mask the error in some way (white stick-on labels for example) and get a correct attempt underway with help. If the child has been too quick for you and the error is already on the page you may:

- allow the child to finish the sentence
- show him how you would write it on the blackboard
- get him to watch and say the word slowly as you slide

a masking card along the word, exposing a letter or letter cluster at a time
- emphasise the matching of sounds and letters.
Note: Accept the child's phonemic analysis (sound analysis) as evidence of the stage he is at.

Re-reading
Get the child to re-read the story pointing word by word. Or re-read his story with him.

Type out the story
Whatever the child writes can be typed out for him to read before too long an interval. A bulletin typewriter (large type) is useful for young readers. The larger type of some typewriters, used with generous spacing is an alternative. DO NOT use capital letters only to solve the type-size problem.

Resist the urge to edit this story or to elaborate it. Change as little of the child's story as is consistent with good teaching. Paste this typed version into the child's unlined exercise book for revision reading.

Record of words written independently
Prepare a list of the child's known words from the Writing Vocabulary test. Keep a record of the new words the child can write without your help, as the child learns them. The following format has been found useful as a record of the build-up of writing vocabulary.

Initial Testing	Wk 1	2	3	4	5	6	7
Name is	the a	I at my	on and me	she in	home do	he	

5 Hearing the Sounds in Words

Introduction
These activities are designed to help the child think about the order of sounds in spoken words, and to help the child to analyse a new word he wants to write into its sequence of sounds.

A beginning programme brings most children to the awareness of sound sequences in words rather effortlessly. However, some children find it extraordinarily difficult to hear the sounds that go to make up words. For example some children consistently focus on the final sound of the word and for them, this completely masks the initial sounds.

For many decades and in many different programmes

teachers have tried to teach children a sound to go with a letter they can see. The children who succeeded in those programmes were able to do just that, and those who failed were probably unable to hear the sound sequences in words anyway.

For children who cannot hear the order of sounds in words the teacher can act as analyser of the words. She articulates the words slowly, but naturally, and gradually develops the same skill in her pupils. It is an essential feature of the theory behind this tutoring to hear sounds in words in sequence. The child's first lessons take place *in the absence of letters or printed words*. The child must *hear* the word spoken, or speak it himself and try to break it into sounds by slowly articulating it. He is asked to show what he can hear with *counters* not *letters*.

Recovery procedures

If a child needs help in hearing the sounds in words he should begin at the beginning of these recovery procedures and work slowly or rapidly through the early stages according to his needs.

Early learning
Establishing the task
In the first few trials the child will be learning what it is the teacher wants him to do. This applies to slow articulation, to clapping or to pushing counters. Take time to get clear what it is you want him to do.

Hearing syllables
Because hearing big chunks of sound is easier than discovering single sounds a good first step is to ask the child to clap the parts he can hear in a few words he knows well. Choose one and two syllable words at first, and later three or four. Repeat this activity from time to time as opportunities arise in connection with reading or writing stories. The activity will help with the longer words he tries to write into his stories.

Hearing the sounds
Prepare for the activities that follow.

• Make a few picture cards for simple words such as *cat*, *bus*, *boy*, *ship*, *house* to use to introduce the task.
• Prepare some cards on which you draw a square for each sound segment in words of two, three and four sounds, for example:

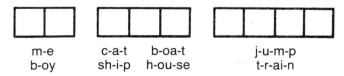

| m-e | c-a-t | b-oa-t | j-u-m-p |
| b-oy | sh-i-p | h-ou-se | t-r-ai-n |

• Have a selection of counters ready.

In the first lessons after the 'roaming around the known' stage only attempt two or three of the activities in the next two lists.

To introduce the slow articulation of words, use a *picture card* and:

• Slowly and deliberately articulate the word for the child. Let him hear the sounds separated but in a natural way.
• Ask the child to articulate the word aloud. Ask him to 'Say it slowly'. This transfers the initiative for the activity to the child.
• Ask the child to watch your lips while you say it, and then to copy you.
• Use a mirror if it helps the child to be more aware of what his lips and tongue are doing.

Use the sound segment cards to make a visual model of the sounds that have been articulated. (Choose a card which has a square for each sound in your demonstration word (i.e. a three square card for c-a-t.) You need a square for every sound in the aural task and NOT for every letter. The transfer to an emphasis on letters comes much later.

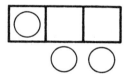

• Model the task for the child. Articulate the word slowly and push the counters into the boxes, sound by sound.
• Now get the child to try this. As long as the child finds the co-ordination of saying slowly and pushing counters too difficult share the task with him. Articulate the word slowly for him while he moves the counters. Or, get the child to articulate slowly while you push the counters. Change roles to enable the child to practise both parts.
• You may guide the child's hand or work alongside him with another card.
• As soon as possible have the child complete the whole task himself. Accept his approximations. Co-ordination will come with practice.

Intermediate steps
Hearing sounds and writing letters
This is an aural task also. The focus is on hearing sounds and clusters of sounds, and finding some way to record them in letters. It helps the child to write words he has not yet learned to write (i.e. spell).

When a child can push counters into the boxes as he says the sounds and when he has a good grasp of letter identification, he is ready to make another kind of model of the sound segments in words, using letters.

Use words the child wants to write in his stories but limit the words for this activity to up to four sounds at first. More than four sounds can be a problem to the beginner. Select activities like those in the following list according to a particular child's needs.

• Articulate the word slowly emphasising the sounds.
• Draw a box for each sound segment on the practice page of the child's writing book.
• Encourage the child to say the word slowly and push counters into the boxes you have drawn. Later he will only need to point to each box as he says the word slowly.
• Ask 'What can you hear? How would you write it? Now where will we put it?' If the child gives the sound but hesitates over writing the letter(s) say 'How would you write it?'
• Accept any sound that the child can hear clearly but cannot write and write it in for him as he watches.
• Let the child record any sound for which he knows the letter but ensure that it goes in the correct box.
• Help the child, if necessary, to make links with what he knows somewhere else — in his alphabet book, or his name, or a word he can already write.
• Provide a magnetic letter or some other model of the letter that the child has forgotten how to write. Let the child who thinks he knows but is unsure do a trial letter on a scrap of paper or write the letter in the air or with his finger on the desk.
• Encourage the child to write the letters he knows.

Use questions like these to locate other letters.

• What else can you hear?
• What do you hear at the beginning?
• What do you hear at the end?
• What do you hear in the middle?

Accept what the child can hear in any order. Do not insist on a beginning to end approach. This will come later, as the child gains control of the task.

The child can record only those letters he knows how to form and the one or two he is currently learning. The teacher can act as his scribe to produce words like these,

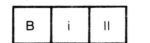
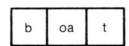

with the child writing only those letters he knows.

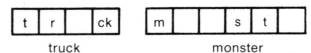

truck   monster

Alternatively, the teacher may get the child to fill in what he can by himself and then complete the word for him, perhaps *teaching one new point* but not explaining everything.

Gradually shift from the question 'What can you hear?' to the question 'What letters would you expect to see?'

A note on consonants and vowels

Be satisfied if he can separate out some of the consonants. Give the child the vowels as these seem to be much more difficult to hear and require more experience with reading and writing.

For the teacher who is not used to a linguist's analysis of the sounds of spoken English *there are traps* in this activity. For example, one child responding well to her own phonemic analysis of *cousins* wrote:

Kusns

Except for the *Ss* which should have been *Zs* this is an accurate rendering of the sounds in the word but not one which helped the child to reach the written form of the word. It was not an appropriate word for training sound to letter analysis.

The teacher must be alert to detect the difference between what is good analysis of sounds and what is confusion or error. Here are some examples of accurate 'hearing' by children which should not be undervalued.

plac   aftr   childrn
(place)   (after)   (children)

Advanced learning
Hearing sounds in words — further transitions
After the early learning and intermediate steps the child is usually able to hear and record the consonants well, has control over writing letters, and is able to select some vowels correctly. He is then ready for an important transition.

I   At this stage we introduce the child to the mismatch between the sounds of the language to which he has been attending and the way we spell the words. Now we want to provide the child with a box for each letter, even though two letters may not represent two sounds.

One of our teachers found an easy way to introduce the transition. She drew enough boxes for the sounds only but she put in a dotted line to divide any box that needed two letters like this:

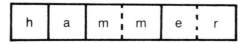

and then gradually transferred to solid lines.

Explain the shift to the child — a box for every letter he needs.

- Articulate the word clearly for the child. Let him hear the segments in sequence several times.
- Make a squared diagram in his booklet with spaces equal to the number of *letters* required.
- Help the child to fill in the letters of the word using stress or pausing on a sound in an exaggerated way to emphasise the sound you want him to focus on.
- As soon as the child can attend to the sound, return to a natural rate and mode of articulation.
- Find similar sound segments in known words.

mot<u>her</u>
mons<u>ter</u>

- Help the child if the word has unusual elements or those that he is not yet ready for (especially vowels).

Sometimes our teachers have provided children with some of the letters for vowels and asked them to select the letter they think could be right. It is not clear how helpful this is.

II Make another special transition as soon as possible. Have the child fill in the letters *in sequence*. This requires him to use new ways of analysing the word he is trying to write.

III As the child becomes a better reader he will still continue to encounter new words and the following activities would still be needed from time to time.

- The child hears the teacher slowly articulating the sounds in sequence, perhaps several times.
- The teacher may ask the child to watch her lips and say it with her.
- The teacher may use a mirror to show the child how she makes the sounds.
- Encourage the child to 'say it slowly'.
- Use stress to emphasise a sound you want him to focus on.
- Use pausing on that sound or draw it out in an exaggerated way to call attention to it.

The writing of the word in boxes will not be needed very often at this stage.

6 Cut-up Stories

Introduction
Cut-up stories provide the child with practice for:

- assembling sentences
- one-to-one correspondence of words spoken and words written

- directional behaviours
- checking behaviours
- breaking oral language into segments
- word study (from occasionally cut-up words).

The puzzle-type task on known text can be used for home practice. The written story in the blank page of the child's exercise book or on the envelope that holds the cut-up words provides a correct model which he may or may not consult, as needs be.

Recovery procedures
The first cut-up stories may be written by the teacher from the child's dictation but usually a teacher asks the child to re-read his story from his unlined book so that she can write it again on light cardboard.

Cut up the story into language units which you know the child will be able to reassemble. Use larger segments for poorer readers. The descending order of size will be phrases, words, structural segments, or clusters of letters, and single letters.

If you want to cut up a word into syllables ask the child to clap the syllables of the word to show you where to cut up the word.

Get the child to reassemble the cut-up story. This usually calls for careful self-monitoring and checking but it can be made easy or difficult. Assembly:

- on top of the model is a matching response — EASY.
- below the model is a matching response — HARDER.
- without the model is a reading response — HARD.

Get the child to scan for errors. If he made errors, say 'Something's not quite right' calling for a self-monitoring response.

Get the child to re-read with careful word by word matching to the syllable level if this was used.

An example at a very early stage
- The child was asked to tell a story.
- The teacher offered to write that story in his book. She wrote it again on light cardboard.
- The child pointed to 'A' and said he could do that one. (The teacher missed the opportunity to have him write what little he knew.)
- The teacher read the written text and modelled pointing behaviour.
- The child tried inaccurately.
- The teacher guided his hand.
- The child tried accurately.
- The teacher did not cut the story into phrases which might have been the appropriate teaching step. She emphasised its word components by reading each word as she chopped it off.

- The child reassembled the story matching it on top of the story in his book. It became a *visual matching* exercise rather than a *reading task*. The last word *bus* was matched but re-oriented 180°.
- The teacher asked him to turn it around and put the tall one on that (left) side. Note that he knew *s* and in *snq* it is correctly oriented.

7 Reading Books

Introduction

There are twin aims achieved in the book reading section of lessons. One is to allow the child scope for practising the orchestration of all the complex range of behaviours he must use, (and this is best achieved on easy or familiar texts). The other is to encourage him to use his reading strategies on novel texts and to support his tentative efforts.

The critical difficulty for some children who seem to have many particular skills and a fair grasp of certain items of knowledge is the using of such assets in the sequential sorting process of reading continuous text. The reading recovery procedures provide three opportunities for fostering integration of skills — in reading text (see below), in writing and re-reading his own stories (see page 63), in reconstructing cut-up versions of those stories (see above).

Recovery procedures

Choice of book

Choose the reading book very carefully. First of all take meaning and language into account. Then from the possible texts select one that is well within the child's control, uses words and letters he knows or can get to using his present strategies. There should be a minimum of new things to learn if the teaching goal is the integration of all these aspects of the task.

Orientation to the story before reading

Introduce the book and make the child familiar with the *plot, the words, the sentences and the writing style*. For example, a teacher might:

- Draw the child's attention to the important ideas.
- Discuss the pictures of the *whole* book.
- Give opportunities for the child to *hear* the new words which he will have to guess from the pictures and language context.
- Ask him to find one to two new and important words in the text after he has said what letter he would expect to see at the beginning.

This effort to facilitate responding, might be explained in terms like recency and familiarity. Another explanation is that the teacher is ensuring that the child has in his head the ideas and the language he needs to produce when prompted in sequence by print cues.

Reading the book with help

Prepared by this the child reads the new material as independently as is possible. (Perhaps only half the book would be read on the first occasion.) The overall aim is to provide opportunities for independent attack and for teacher confirmation and reinforcement of appropriate behaviours.

Encourage strong, definite locating behaviours getting the child to point to each word with the index finger to achieve crisp word-by-word integration of point-say-look behaviours.

Support the child with any particular features that are likely to cause him difficulty. For example, provide a model which emphasises by stress, shouting, singing or some other means the anticipated difficulty. In this example *early* was expected to present a particular child with a problem.

> The daisy is asleep
> EARLY in the morning.

Or with minimum help

With a child who is using cues appropriately from all areas, and is on the way to independence say, '*I want you to look at all the pictures and tell me what the story is about. Then I want you to read it all by yourself. I am not going to help unless you really can't do it.*'

Accompany the child's pointing with your own pointer and fail to move on when he makes an error that you see he could self-correct. Sound the initial letter if necessary.

Comment positively when the child corrects himself. Reinforce self-correction especially if the child tries to use the kind of cue he has previously avoided. Talk about self-correction. Say how much you like it.

Second reading for fluency

Re-read the story with the child, for a second time in the *same lesson* to get fluency and a flow of words. Hopefully time will allow for this. As you read stay one step behind the child on problem words to check his mastery of them.

Home and school practice

Accumulate a box of familiar books and re-read a selection of these each session, say two at the beginning of the lesson. The practice encourages confidence and fluency in bringing reading behaviours together. Get the child to read easy books at home for independent practice.

A child who is on the way to independence needs as many books as possible at his level. Allow the child to learn to read by reading many books.

Re-reading of the book

When a book has been introduced and read once be ready to check it for accuracy at the next session. Check out any remaining errors with word analysis exercises such as:

- use of structural features, s, ed, ing
- matching with finger
- segmenting the sentence or word
- asking 'What letters do you expect to see?'

Here is an example of a check on a known book.

- The teacher reads the title, *Who are you?* and asks the child to read it with his finger. The teacher can observe directional behaviour and speech-to-print matching. The child is invited to organise and control his own reading behaviour independently.
- The child reads the book and the teacher takes a Running Record.
- The child reads *bears* for *elephants* and corrects himself. The teacher says, '*What does elephants start with?*' an invitation for aural analysis of *e* in *elephants* and a sound-to-letter association.
- The teacher quickly checks some knowledge of individual words which were teaching points for this book. She uses a sliding mask card to effeciently and swiftly isolate the word, and asks '*What is that?*' The child responds with speed. She includes a question about punctuation, *a question mark*.
- This book is placed in the child's box of books he has read.

8 Learning to Look at Print

Introduction

The eye does not photograph the detail of print and transfer it to the brain. The child must learn to attend to print detail in certain orders for letters, and for words. Some children, finding this difficult or tedious, coast along on their language skills and pay as little attention to the detail of print as they can get away with.

A child who only knows a few letters and words is probably not using visual signposts or cues. Ways of looking at print and searching for cues must be established. Most children will discover all that they need to know as they read books. A few children take a very passive approach to print. They need more help in learning about print.

Recovery procedures

Looking at print — early learning
Start from the known and move out very slowly to anything new.

The known will be:

- the child's name
- a few words which he can read and/or write
- one or two particular books
- the child's dictated story.

From the focus of the child's vocabulary the teaching can slowly move towards extending the child on each activity above.

Here is a first lesson in a recovery programme built around the child's name. The teacher uses three ways of directing the child's attention to visual features of print.

The teacher says '*Make your name here,*' but the child makes no response. The teacher begins to write the child's name.

She pays attention to the first letter, saying, '*We make it like this.*'

She models the movements vertically in the air.

Three ways of remembering

1	Movement	The teacher holds the child's hand and guides him. This identifies the letters by *movement*.
2	Words	'*Down and around*' she says. This is a *verbal* description of movement.
3	Visual Form	She writes the letter in his book. She may ask the child to write it. This is a *visual* model.

The teacher writes the rest of the child's name and he copies this. From this the child learns some specific letters:

- how to put them in a set sequence
- several features of letters, usable in other letters
- several features of words.

Suggestions for extending his knowledge of words

- Have the child make a word out of magnetic letters. Jumble it and remake it until the child can do this fluently.
- Write the word in big print for him.
- Ask the child to trace the word with finger contact saying each part of the word as he traces it.
- Use a paint-brush and water to make a disappearing word on the blackboard.
- Use a wet crayon to make a magic 'appearing' word on the blackboard.

The next suggestion is a very important one.

- Ask the child to write the word many times getting fluency and overlearning.
- Keep these words in mind to use in other activities.

Gradually extend the child's writing vocabulary. A useful initial vocabulary can be selected from:

Child's name, I, a, is, in, am, to, come, like, see, the, my, we, and, at, here, on, up, look, go, this, it, me.

These words help with the stories the child tries to write and with the first books he can read. Try to keep all words within the vocabulary that he controls, and slowly add to this.

Reading recovery teachers have found it useful to build up vocabulary charts for individual children, to be read, referred to, and added to during lessons.

Another idea is to build up a box of word cards indexed by letters of the alphabet. Such a *collection of partly-known words* has several uses.

• It provides a child-sized concept of what he is trying to master.
• It helps him to remember a word, that is, it is a retrieval device.
• It reminds the teacher of earlier work the child has done. Known words and words that prove unmanageable can be withdrawn (discreetly) from the collection.

Suggestions for extending his knowledge of letters

At first use only the letters the child can already identify. Give him lots of practice with these.

• Allow the child to label letters in *any* appropriate way — by name, by sound, or by word beginning. We find good readers use all three ways of identifying letters. It seems to be useful to have more than one way of labelling a letter, and we suggest that you do not insist on only one type of label being used.
• Have the child run over the new letter with his finger to feel the shape. Identify the letter by name. Talk about the similarity/dissimilarity of the capital and lower case forms.
• Model the formation of the new letter with chalk on the blackboard writing in large print and directing the movements verbally.
• Giving him verbal instructions, and guiding his hand if necessary, have the child write the letter:

- in the air
- on the blackboard
- on paper.

Teachers in our programme developed many interesting activities for drawing children's attention to the features of letters such as sticky coloured paper cut-outs, formation cards showing where to start letters, tracing paper activities, and so on. Only do what is essential. Do not get too focussed on letters.

Work for flexibility.

• Use vertical and horizontal surfaces.
• Use different mediums — felt pen, chalk, magnetic letters.
• For a particular child use unusual mediums — sandpaper or felt letters.
• Use different sizes of print.
• Look for a simple book that illustrates the new letter (such as a Price-Milburn skill builder) and read through it, emphasising the initial sounds.
• Get the child to identify the letter by an object which he identifies with the new letter. (It might be a picture from the book.)
• Go through his alphabet book (see the end of this section) to show him where the new letter fits in sequence and draw the key picture and the letter forms.
• Teach a new word starting with that letter.

Every new thing learned should be revised in several other activities.

When children confuse letters

Some children have well-established habits of confusing letters. One way to help them control and monitor these unwanted responses on the one hand, and develop the desirable new responses on the other, is to bring the behaviour under verbal direction for a short time. This practice must be used sensitively. It is a temporary device which, if continued too long will itself become an unwanted response, slowing up the automatic responding required.

• Attend to similarities and differences of letters.
• Use three-dimensional forms such as magnetic letters and create clear demonstrations of any distinctions that the child should learn.
• Put three or four examples of the same letter onto the magnetic board. Jumble the forms with some known letters and have the child find 'all the *E*s' and put them in a line.

Because it takes reading recovery children some time to distinguish letters revise new learning frequently. As they become very familiar with some letters those letters can be omitted from the practice exercises.

There are many ways in which letters can be paired, and grouped. Games can be invented to suit particular children, but don't waste time on unnecessary games.

Attend to the forming of letters which are confused

Draw the child a model on the blackboard slowly, directing the movements verbally. Ask the child to try, and guide his hand if necessary. Verbalise the movement (e.g. *'Make k down, and in and out'*). Try to bring the child's movements under your verbal control and then transfer this verbal control to the child. Continue to practise after the child gives the correct response and revise often.

Attend to common faults

The child sometimes adopts an awkward starting position, for example. If this is important direct attention to it. Be firm about essentials, that is, whatever your most important teaching points are, ignore other inadequacies. You cannot afford to overteach on non-essentials. It costs too much in motivation.

Letter names

You may direct the child's attention to movement or to visual shape. But if you want to talk about the letters it usually helps to use letter names. They seem to act as a shorthand type of label representing many other experiences with letters.

Three important points

Letter learning for most children is done incidentally as they learn to read stories. Special help with letter learning for reading recovery children must not become an end in itself. It is a minor part of a recovery programme. The child cannot afford to waste time on letter games when he could be reading well-chosen books. Careful judgement is needed to give the child just enough opportunity to gain control of letter identification.

In many cases of letter confusion an appropriate strategy is to help the child gain control of *one* of the confusing letters before introducing the second. It does not help most children to work on confusing letters side by side.

The aim is to have a child recognise letters as rapidly as we do without any props. He needs to end up with a fast recognition response. Be careful that your teaching leads to this.

An alphabet book

Early learning

It is usually desirable to take stock of and tidy up a child's knowledge of the alphabet. One idea that works well with children having difficulty is to make a paper book which will allow the alphabet to be printed in sequence, with a drawing for each letter the child knows. Use the form of the letter that the child already knows, capital or lower case.

When a child knows more than 10 letters write *these letters only* in the alphabet book leaving gaps for letters yet to be learned. Use a key picture which the child himself identifies with that letter already.

The child has a feel for the size of the task, how far he has gone, what he knows for certain and as the letters not yet known are flipped over, he must feel that it is important to be sure of and use what he knows and to overlook for the present, some of the difficulties.

The child's own alphabet book has proved more useful than published books we have tried. Yet for the child having little difficulty with reading, a beautifully illustrated alphabet book would be an enriching experience.

Advanced learning

When the child has fairly extensive control over letter knowledge practise sequencing the alphabet by getting him to give the consecutive letter before you turn to that page.

Teacher (pointing):   a — apple
Child (anticipating):   b — balloon
                            (*Turn the page*)

Teacher (pointing):   c — cat
Child (anticipating):   d — dog
                            (*Turn the page*)

Avoid saying '*a is for apple*' because many children try to find a printed sign for *is for*.

I have been asked 'What contribution does knowing the letter names make, apart from providing a metalanguage for talking about print?' Firstly, it is very helpful to have a way of talking about these small units of print — this level of print organisation. Secondly the collection has very little use except that it provides the child with a record, or collection, or inventory of the reference points to which he can anchor his current efforts. Thirdly it provides the detail of the journey taken and a map of the length of journey yet to be taken.

9 Teaching for Operations or Strategies

Introduction

On new or novel texts children have to engage in 'reading work'. This is where they increase their power over the reading task. They solve their problems by using their theories of the world and their theories of written language. They cross-check in their heads which options are most likely. This reading work can be *heard* in the early stages of reading progress but it becomes a silent process. These monitoring and problem-solving strategies or operations going on in the child's head are more powerful than some of the weaker, overt procedures that teachers have encouraged children to use, like sounding out the word or reading on.

Good readers
Reading instruction often focusses on items of knowledge — words, letters, sounds. Most children respond to this teaching in active ways. They search for links between the items and they relate new discoveries to old knowledge. They operate on print as Piaget's children operate on problems, searching for relationships which order the complexity of print and therefore simplify it. For such children the teaching sequence described in these teaching procedures is unnecessary.

Poor readers
Children who fail to progress in reading do not approach print in this way. The operations which they have tried to carry out have not brought order to the complexity and they have often become passive in their confusion.

This section offers suggestions which have proved useful in getting passive poor readers to become more active in searching for cues, predicting possible responses and verifying these responses.

A self-improving system
The end-point of such instruction is reached when children have a self-improving system — a set of operations just adequate for reading a slightly more difficult text for the precise words and meanings of the author.

When we operate or work on a problem we are engaged in a conscious search for solutions. In reading we sometimes consciously search for a word or a meaning or a correction but most of the time our active search is a fast reaction of the brain that seems to be automatic and not conscious. Perhaps strategies is a better name for these fast reactions used while reading.

Recovery procedures: operations or strategies used on texts
A child can only acquire and practise these important operations or strategies on texts as he reads books and re-reads the stories he has written. The earliest strategies (1-4) are simple. They are important because through them the child comes to control his visual attention to print. These earliest strategies give the child a means of checking that he is attending to the right part of the page. They are:

1   Directional movement
  Ideas for encouraging appropriate directional behaviours have been described already under Learning About Direction (page 60).

2   One to one matching
  This was discussed in detail under Locating Responses

(page 61). Here are some ways to encourage this as the child reads books.

 • Say '*Read it with your finger.*'
   Or '*Did that match?*'
   Or '*Were there enough words?*'
   Or '*Did you run out?*'
 • Accompany the child's pointing with your own pointer and fail to move on when he makes an error that you feel he could self-correct.
 • When you want to slow down a too-fluent language response, use two small pieces of card or two fingers to frame each word.

3   Locate one or two known words
After the child has read the text encourage him to locate items he knows in the text.

 • Read back an error sentence to him and ask '*Is that right?*'
 • Re-read the previous word or words with fluent phrasing and stop at the problem word.
 • Re-read the previous phrase leading up to the problem word fluently, and articulate the first sound of the problem word.

4   Locate an unknown word
As in (3) above.

Be careful not to establish a pattern where the child waits for the teacher to do the work. This is the point at which the child must learn that he must work at a difficulty, take some initiative, make some links. It is the general principle that needs to be established at this time and it does not matter which type of cues the child uses. Different children will use different types, depending upon what is easy for them at this time.

5   Prompt the child to use a special cue he knows
This may be any type of cue. The aim is to have the child take some initiative and do some 'reading work'. You should welcome any contribution the child can make to solving the problem.

6   Give the child the new word
Follow this modelling with a question like:

 • Would that make sense?
 • Would 'help' fit there?
 • Do you think it looks like 'help'?

Checking on oneself or self-monitoring
The successful reader who is making no errors is monitoring his reading at all times. Effective monitoring is a highly skilled process constructed over many years of

reading. It begins early but must be continually adapted to encompass new challenges in texts.

• To encourage self-monitoring in the very early stages ask the child to go back to one to one pointing:
Say '*Point to each one.*'
Or '*Use a pointer and make them match.*'
• Direct the child's attention to meaning:
Say '*Look at the picture.*'
Or '*What happened in the story when...*'
• For particular attention to an error allow the child to continue to the end of the sentence:
Say '*I liked the way you did that.*
        But can you find the hard bit?'
Or '*I liked the way you did that.*
        You found the hard bit.
        Where was it?'
• If the child gives signs of uncertainty — hesitation, frowning, a little shake of the head — even though he takes no action:
Say '*Was that OK?*'
Or '*Why did you stop?*'
Or '*What did you notice?*'

These questions tell the child that you want him to monitor his own reading. The operation to be learned is checking on oneself. It is more important that the child comes to check on his own behaviour than that he be required to use all the sources of cues at this stage.

• Don't forget to reinforce the child for his self-monitoring attempts whether they are successful or not.
Say '*I liked the way you tried to work that out.*'
• Cues from letter sequences. Let the child predict the word he expects it to be. Cover the problem word and ask for something you know he knows about that word. One of these questions might be useful.
'*What do you expect to see at the beginning?*
        at the end?
        after the 'M'?'
Then ask him to check as you uncover the word.
• Ask the child 'Were you right?' after both *correct* and *incorrect* words. Ask 'How did you know?' after correct words.
• As the child becomes more skilled do less teaching and prompting and modelling. Merely say 'Try that again' but make sure that your voice carries two messages. You are requiring him to search, because you know he can, and you are confident he can solve the problem.

Cross-checking

When the child can monitor his own reading and can search for and use structure or message or sound cues or visual cues, begin to encourage him to check one kind of cue against another.

• Point up discrepancies between two sources of cues.
Say '*It could be... but look at...*'
• Or insert possible words until the child can confirm the response using initial and final letters.
• Or say '*Check to see if what you read looks right and sounds right to you.*'

An example of fostering checking behaviour
T: '*What was the new word you read?*'
Ch: '*Bicycle*'
T: '*How did you know it was bicycle?*'
Ch: '*It was a bike*' (semantics)
T: '*What did you expect to see?*'
Ch: '*A "b"?*'
T: '*What else?*'
Ch: '*A little word, but it wasn't*'
T: '*So, what did you do?*'
Ch: '*I thought of bicycle*'
T: (Reinforcing the checking)
'*Good, I liked the way you worked at that all by yourself.*'

Outcome — The child will attend to checking because the teacher attended to it.

Searching for cues

To develop the child's abilities to search for all types of cues use the following set of questions in flexible ways. In your first attempts to call, say, structure to the child's attention use the child's present behaviour in your first examples.

• Cues in sentence structure (syntax):
Say '*You said... Does that sound right?*'
Or '*Can you say it that way?*'
• Cues from the message (semantics):
Say '*You said... Does that make sense?*'
• Cues from the letters (graphic cues):
Say '*Does it look right?*'
• Or more generally:
Say '*What's wrong?*'

If the child has a bias towards letter detail the teacher's prompts will be directed towards the message and the language structure.

• She may need to orient the child to the picture as a meaning source.
• She may need to induce the word as when the problem word was broth and the teacher said, '*There was an old lady who lived in a shoe...*' and the child said, '*I know — soup!*'
• Sometimes it is necessary for a child to gain control over a particular language structure first, so that he can bring it back to the reading situation.

Four types of cue

From the theory of reading behind these recovery procedures there are four types of cue any two of which may be cross-checked to confirm a response. They can be represented by a square.

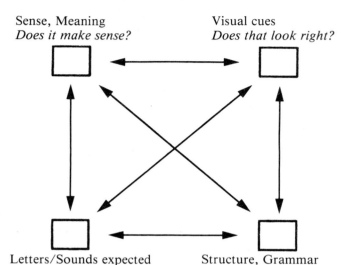

Sense, Meaning
Does it make sense?

Visual cues
Does that look right?

Letters/Sounds expected
What would you expect to see?

Structure, Grammar
Can we say it that way?

An example of fostering searching behaviour

T: *You almost got that page right. There was something wrong with this line. See if you can find what was wrong.'*

Ch: (Child silently re-reads checking)
'I said Lizard but it's Lizard's.'

T: *'How did you know?'*

Ch: *'Cause it's got an "s".'*

T: *'Is there any other way we could know?'* (Search further)

Ch: (Child re-runs in whisper)
'It's funny to say "Lizard dinner"!
It has to be Lizard's dinner like Peter's dinner, doesn't it?'

T: (Reinforcing the searching)
'Yes. That was good. You found two ways to check on that tricky new word.'

Outcome — The child will attend to searching because the teacher attended to it.

Self-correction

The child who monitors his own reading, searches for cues and cross-checks at least two types of information, will be self-correcting some of his own errors.

• Comment positively on self-correction. Say *'I liked the way you found out what was wrong all by yourself.'*
• Allow time for self-correction. The child must take the initiative.

• To make a child even more independent of the teacher don't do anything when he makes a mistake or stops. Don't give him any clues. Say *'You made a mistake on that page. Can you find it?'* This places the responsibility on the child.

A note on verbalising the process

Check on some words accurately read with *'How did you know?'* or *'Were you right?'*

In familiar tasks a young child often comes to a stage where he can comment on what he can do. The question *'How did you know it was X?'* invites the child to examine his own behaviour, after he has successfully carried out some operation in his reading. The teacher may know what cues he used and may want him to verbalise this. Or she may be asking for the child's help so that she can understand this particular strength he has.

What is the relationship between the need for fast, automatic responses to words and phrases, and this instructional device which slows up the process and asks the child to think about it? It seems legitimate to encourage a child to verbalise a strategy or a principle or a rule-like consistency because these have more general application. They have generative value. It also seems legitimate to bring to a child's notice a success he has had in mastering a previously difficulty, because confidence has generative value also.

It is a tactic that could be overworked and could interfere with the automatic responding that goes with fluency.

The goal is a self-improving system

Teachers aim to produce independent readers whose reading improves whenever they read. In independent readers:

• early strategies are secure and habituated
• the child *monitors* his own reading
• he *searches* for cues in word sequences, in meaning, in letter sequences
• he *discovers* new things for himself
• he *cross-checks* one source of cues with another
• he *repeats* as if to *confirm* his reading so far
• he *self-corrects* assuming the initiative for making cues match
• he *solves* new words by these means (see also page 77).

Extending these operations

As the child reaches out to more complex texts and writes longer and more involved stories these operations will be used with increasing speed and fluency on:
• longer stretches of meaning
• less familiar language
• less predictable texts.

10 Linking Sound Sequence with Letter Sequence

Introduction

There is an exact co-ordination needed by the skilled reader between what his eye is attending to and what he is saying. (More precisely that should read what his eye has just been attending to and what he is now saying, because his eyes will have moved on to pick up the next set of visual cues.)

In earlier sections ideas were introduced for developing:

A the analysis of sounds in spoken words (auditory) and
B the analysis of signs in written words (visual).

Reading recovery teachers found children who could do **A** but not **B** and vice versa.

They also found children who could do both **A** and **B** as separate activities but who could not link one with the other. The activities listed below were found useful in developing links between *how the child analyses the sounds of words he needs to write or to check in his reading* and *how the child analyses the letters and letter clusters in a word in his reading against the word he is trying to say*.

As we came to understand these problems we learned that this was not a simple problem of phonics. This was an inability to co-ordinate two complex sets of operations — sound sequence analysis and letter sequence analysis.

In many classrooms around the world while teachers have been teaching phonics competently children have probably been learning something much more useful. They have been constructing the complex associations between sound sequences and letter sequences that enable us to become fluent readers.

We found children who needed extra help to begin to make these links for themselves. Once they understood the nature of the task they began to teach themselves in ways that were more efficient than any instruction programme could hope to be.

If the child can move easily from sounds to letters or from letters to sounds he is easily prompted by the teacher.

Check to see if what you read looks right and sounds right to you. Some children are unable to initiate such checks.

Recovery procedures

If the child finds it hard to go from sounds to letters
In his reading a child may focus on letters and be able to remember the sounds they make and yet that child may find it difficult to go from hearing the sounds in words to producing the letters he needs to represent those sounds in his writing.

Hearing the sounds in words
Get the child to articulate the word he wants to write slowly, pushing counters into boxes in the word diagram for each sound he can hear described earlier (see page 65). Help him to fill in the boxes.

Make and say
• If the word is a high frequency word, that he cannot yet write, ask him what he would expect to see at the beginning, and/or the end, and/or the middle.
• Give him the correct magnetic letters and ask him to make it on the magnetic board. Make him construct the word several times to get the sequence right.
• Say '*Look at the word. Say it slowly and run your finger across it.*'
• Ask him to close his eyes and say to him '*Can you see it?*'
• Ask him to write it without looking.
• Write it several times to get overlearning.

What does he expect to see
• Ask the child to locate a particular interest word in a new reading text *after* he has said what he would expect to see at the beginning.
• Get him to confirm or discount miscues in his reading by covering the problem word and getting him to say what he would expect to see at the beginning, at the end, in the middle and then asking him to check visually. The aim is to get him to engage in independent monitoring of his own attempts and to develop revision through checking.

If the child finds it hard to go from letters to sounds
A child may be able to analyse sounds to letters in his writing and with the help of word boxes but may not be able to use letter-to-sound associations to help him eliminate miscues in his reading.

Using his own stories
• Get the child to remake his own stories that have been rewritten on paper strips and cut up. The sounds of the story are in his head and he uses these as a guide to finding the words he has written.
• Ask the child to clap syllables and show him where to cut a word into two parts. Then get him to remake the story.

On books
• When the child comes to a problem word in the text, sound the initial letter for him to help him to predict what the right word might be. Then transfer this sounding task to him by getting him to attend to the initial letter or letters and to get his mouth ready to say it.

The aim is to make him more conscious of a strategy that will help him to eliminate the words that would fit the context but not the first letter cues.

• If he has good mastery of sound-to-letter analysis but yet does not independently attempt some analysis of simple words in text, write them letter by letter on the blackboard, getting him to articulate the accumulating letters until the word that would fit the context comes into his head — *c   cr   cra   crash.*

Making this operation more explicit

Check on some words accurately read with '*How did you know?*' or '*Were you right?*'

In reading instruction, this invites the child to examine his own behaviour after he has successfully applied the necessary operations to his reading. For example:

The child read *from* as *for* in a sentence and corrected himself.
The teacher asked '*Is it from?*'
The child replied '*It starts with f.*'
The teacher said '*So does for.*'
The child said '*It ends with m.*'

It seems legitimate to encourage a child to verbalise these operations from time to time as a check on what he is doing. Verbalising is a tactic that could be overworked however, and could interfere with the automatic responding that is required for fluency. (See also page 78.)

11 Teaching for Word Analysis

Introduction

Most schemes for teaching word analysis begin with the assumptions that:

• the teacher needs an instructional sequence
• this can be arrived at by some logical ordering process.

In these reading recovery procedures we have assumed that the goal of tutoring is to achieve the most rapid acceleration possible for the child, and, therefore:

• that the child's skills should determine the sequence
• that the word segments attended to should be those used by good readers at this level of learning to read
• that the sequence should be ordered by psychological rather than logical factors.

Following these assumptions and referring to research on early reading and to Elkonin's work we have found that *initial letters* or *final letters* are the starting points for a child's detailed analysis of words and that quite rapidly he goes beyond this to *easy-to-hear consonants within a word, easy-to-hear vowels and other consonants and hard-to-hear vowels.*

If the child is writing stories and doing an efficient sound

to letter analysis of the new words he wants to write, the problem to be faced by the teaching procedures in this section is — *Does he attempt a left-to-right analysis of new words in his reading?*

But, good readers read in chunks. They attach sounds to a group of letters (rather than each letter) if that works. So the child's attention should be directed to the largest chunks or groups of letters within words that will achieve the analysis. This aim conflicts with many reading programmes which insist on directing the child's attention to the smallest units.

Recovery procedures for word analysis

Initial letters or signs

Draw attention to initial letters:

• Words that begin with the same sound — *Frank, father, Harry, here.*
• Confusable words with different first letters — *smoke, firemen, hose.*
• Go from first letter to sound.
• Go from sound to expected first letter.
• Go from first letter sound to predict the word and say '*What else could you check?*'
• What do initial 'speech marks' tell you?
• Deal with capital/lower case contrasts — *Going, going, Is, is.*

Final letters or signs

Draw attention to final letters:

• The presence of *s* — plural *trees*, possessive *Lizard's*, verb *jumps.*
• The absence of *s*.
• Punctuation — full-stop, questions, exclamations, speech marks.
• Final letters in words — *it, in, his, him, but, bun, bus, buzz.*

First steps in word study

The child has to discover the significant features in a word that will allow him to recognise it another time. Word building or writing can help him do this.

When a child can build a word, slowly but correctly, give him three or more opportunities to:

• do it again
• do it more quickly
• do it another way
• do it in another place
• do it fast.

These encourage habituation of the response, over-learning that resists forgetting, automatic responding and flexibility.

• Use magnetic letters for building, dismembering, and reforming words. The actions needed for this help to make many points about letter sequences.
• Use chalk and blackboard for rewriting a word many times.
• Use a larger than usual print with a felt pen.
• Use a paintbrush and water on a blackboard.
• Use written words cut into two or three pieces.
• Use word cards for practice and revision *only after learning has occurred.*

Some distinctions that are needed for early reading books are:

• Between pairs in these groups.
this, the	*that, then*
and, am	*at, a*
me, we	*he, she*
• Between capital and lower case pairs.
| *Here, here* | *In, in* |
| *Is, is* | *And, and* |
• Between proper names when needed.
Andrew, Ann
• Between confusions as they arise.
| *Here, the* | *a, the* |
| *am, on* | *help, play* |
• Between words only as needed for the particular texts
shouted / said.

In addition to the necessary distinctions spend some time on word building from the child's repertoire.
baby, bird, bee
struck, duck, luck, muck
cat, can, came
big, bag, bug
fast, first, feast

Preparing for using letter groups or 'chunks' of information
Hearing the breaks: clapping two- and three-syllable words
As opportunities arise with multisyllabic words ask the child to clap the syllables.
jum / bo / jet	*stick / ing*
el / e / phant	*plast / er*
Pe / ter	*hip / po / pot / a / mus*
go / ing	*mo / ther*

Distinguishing similar words
A   Related to a topic.
B   With similar components.
Use opportunities as they arise such as
space / man	*up / stairs*
space / ship	*down / stairs*
fire / men	*in / to*
fire / engine	*to / day*

Encourage flexibility in thinking about letters and letter groups in words. Have the child build words from magnetic letters.

Say   *'Use two letters to make one word.'*
Or   *'Use three letters to make one word.'*
Or   *'Use four letters to make one word.'*
Ask   *'How many letters are in your word?'*
      'Show me a letter. Show me a word.'

Engage in as much word building with magnetic letters as is needed to foster the visual analysis of words in text.
The manipulation in constructing words, in breaking up words, and in substituting letters is important for reading recovery children.

am, Sam, Ham, ham
father, mother, sister, water, her, over
look-s, -ed, -ing
like-s, -ed
play-s, -ed, ing
go, going
play, please

When the child begins to indicate such analysis for himself during text reading this word building with magnetic letters is only used for a particular teaching point.
The visual analysis of words in text can be encouraged by the teacher's questions as the child reads text.

• After success in word solving.
Say *'How did you know it was. . .?'*
• When the child stops at a new word.
Say *'What could you try. . .?'*
Or *'Do you know a word like that?'*
Or *'What would you think it could be?'*
Or *'Do you know a word that starts with those letters?'*
Or *'Do you know something that ends with those letters?'*
Or *'What do you know that might help?'*

An example of fostering the use of letter clusters
The child, reading the word *joking*, stops.
T :   *'What does it start with?'*
Ch :   *'j'*
T :   *'Can you say more than that?'*
Ch :   *'jo — k . . . joke'*
T :   *'Is the end of joke right?'*
Ch :   *'ing . . . joking'*
T :   *'Yes. You found two parts to that word, jok and ing. We could look at other words like that*
      pok   ing
      tak   ing
      hik   ing
Let's go on with the story.'

Outcome — The value of using letter clusters has been stressed.

The usual analysis of words into useful letter clusters will also be developed in the Writing Stories exercises and associated sound-to-letter analyses. The child will want to hurriedly write down the clusters he knows, resisting a teacher's attempts to get him to work letter by letter. And rightly so.

Teaching and testing for control of letter groups

This is done in a task like the Writing Vocabulary Test. The child is asked to write some words he knows and as opportunities arise he is asked to write another word differing in one letter or letter cluster from the one he has already written. Two or three substitutions of this kind can be asked for.

This is very similar to the word-constructing and letter-substituting tasks he used to do with magnetic letters but it is harder in this 'spelling exercise' form.

12 Teaching for Phrasing and Fluency

Encourage the child to read familiar text quickly. Say '*Can you read this quickly,*' or '*Put them all together so that it sounds like talking*'.

Insist that the child pause appropriately, especially at full-stops and speech marks. Say '*Read the punctuation*'.

Read a story to the child; re-read it with the child emphasising the phrasing. This should provide support from the feel and the sound of the patterns of words and breaks or pauses.

Write down a repetitive sentence or phrase from a specially selected story and treat it like the story described above.

Especially with direct speech ask the child to read it as he would if he was in that situation. For example, '*I'll eat you up.*'

Use known texts, or texts with rhythm-like songs and poems (or sometimes prose) because they carry the reader forward.

Mask the text with a card, or your thumb and expose two or three words at a time asking the child to '*Read it all*'.

Use an overhead projector, masking the text and pacing the child as you expose some for him to read.

Slide a card underneath each line if you wish to discourage word by word reading, finger pointing or voice pointing.

Slide a card over the text forcing the child's pace so he processes a little more fluently without breaking down. This encourages him to make his eyes work ahead of his voice.

13 Teaching for a Sequencing Problem

Introduction

Although the skilled reader may not attend to cues in print in a strictly left to right order, that is how our written code is organised and children have to be able to attend to cues in sequence. Children have difficulty with this for two quite different reasons. Some find it very difficult to control the steady letter by letter analysis sometimes required of them and they adopt a haphazard approach because it is easier. Others could exercise the required control but they prefer a more interesting, varied approach and resist the attempt to confine their processing to a more orderly procedure. A sequencing problem may be caused by lack of feeling for direction or by poor checking skills for maintaining consistency. It occurs in children who have some elementary reading skills.

Recovery procedures

1   Have the child construct a tricky word out of ready-made (magnetic) letters.
    Say '*Once more, as fast as you can,*' encouraging several attempts to provide practice for doing this fluently.
2   Have the child write a word in an unlined book several times. Say '*Once more as fast as you can,*' encouraging correct and fluent performance. Write this word in a sentence in an unlined book.
3   Use word building, word demolition, and reconstruction, making new words with substitution of magnetic letters.
4   Practise word-construction letter by letter on the blackboard in a word diagram. (See sound segmentation page 65.)
    '*What can you hear at the beginning?*'
    '*What can you hear at the end?*'

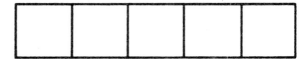

Articulate carefully letter by letter for the child so that you lengthen the particular letter he is working out.

Have the child reconstruct a cut-up child-dictated sentence which the teacher has written. Gradually as the child improves direct his attention to finer detail in the following order:

A   Phrasing.
B   Words.
C   Small segments — obvious syllables, endings, common consonant clusters, vowel-consonant clusters (s — and).

The challenge is to maintain sequence despite the attention to detail.

Have at hand masking cards with windows of various sizes to expose segments or groups of units to be attended to. (This is a visual attending device but can also be used to foster correct sequencing.) Use these on text as the child reads or following a page where a difficulty occurred.

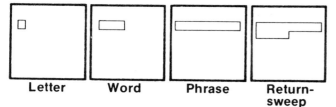

| Letter | Word | Phrase | Return-sweep |

Mask a problem word in text and exposing a sound unit at a time, have the child blend these in the correct sequence.

14 Strong Skills Which Block Learning

Introduction

If some inappropriate reading skill or responses to a particular item become overlearned and fluent they are hard to unlearn. Some guidelines are:

• Prevent the inappropriate behaviour occurring whenever possible.
• Penetrate the old pattern by splitting it apart — over space and over time.
• Use exaggeration by shouting, by stress, by elaborate acting, singing in the manner of recitative, and so on.
• Move with large movements before refining the pattern.
• Aim to get flexibility, and alternative operations established.
• Move cautiously towards fluency. The child may manage to control a new response by thinking about it, and although this makes for slow responding, he may then be able to control the old rapid, unthinking, response.

Sometimes children fail to integrate cues from different sources because they tend to focus on one kind of cue ignoring discrepancies in the other types of cue.

As the child reads, his teacher's confirmation of his successful processing, and the nature of her prompts become important ways of focussing the child's attention on neglected areas.

What is the teacher's purpose in the questions she uses when she prompts? Probably she has several different kinds of prompts. Sometimes she invites the child to think about meaning as in:

Where do you think the bear lives? (Target word: *cave*)

At other times the prompt may be to check something, like a previous sentence or a re-run of the present sentence (perhaps it was sleeping in the...).

Another kind of leading question may point the reader towards letter/sound cues, like '*What sounds can you see in that word?*' or '*Get your mouth ready for the first sound.*'

And yet another strategy may be to encourage the child to solve the word by analogy with a more frequently used word. This is sometimes difficult, and *cave* is an example of such difficulty.

If a teacher specialises in one type of prompting or cueing the child will tend to specialise (through deprivation of alternative opportunities) and will not achieve flexibility in his use of strategies.

If the child has a bias towards the use of language cues, the teacher's prompts will be directed to either a strong locating response (she may ask him to '*Try that again with your finger*') or to print detail (she may get the child to confirm a prompt by attending to initial and final letters firstly in the spoken word and then in the written word).

15 When it is Hard to Remember

Introduction

Some children have particular difficulty in calling up an association of a label for a word, or a name for a letter or the names for story characters. I refer here to children who have difficulty with recall on most occasions, not merely a temporary lapse. This low recall means that the earliest, easiest and most basic links of oral language with print are very difficult for the child to establish. Some of the following approaches may help. The teaching goal is to develop strategies for remembering or recalling rather than merely forcing a particular association into the child's mind.

Recovery procedures

Use the child's association

When Paul knew very few letters he never had difficulty with O.

    O for Oboe

For him that was easy; for another child it would have been impossible.

Mark had trouble with G. After several weeks his teacher found an appropriate meaningful association that triggered the letter name. By calling part of the symbol a saddle she taught Mark to say '*A saddle for the gee-gee.*'

Arrange for repetition
Increase the opportunities to recall, that is to use strategies for remembering, on a few very important items. Practise recall on known items.

Arrange for overlearning
This refers to the practice we get after something has been learned. It is an insurance against forgetting.

Continue to provide opportunities for further practice long after the labels or names seem to have been learned.

Use games
Sometimes a game like '*Snap*', or matching face-down cards is useful for providing both practice and the expectation that one has to remember.

Revise
Regularly go back to old difficulties and check that they have been established by repetition and overlearning.

Teach for flexibility
Use:
1   different responses like singing, shouting, or role-playing suitable actions, as for oboe, or gee-gee.
2   different mediums such as magnetic letters, chalk, felt-tip pens, paint, cards, slide-projection.

Extend the known set
Have several cards of all the letters/words that the child recognises plus the ones that are half-known plus one or two that have just been taught. Run through these making 'your pile' and 'my pile' of the known and not known words.

Games can be adapted for the purpose of increasing the items that a child remembers. For example, in '*Fishing*', the teacher makes several cards of each of the words that the child knows with upper and lower case versions. The game is to form pairs by asking your partner if he has a word that you have in your hand.

'*Do you have go?*'
'*Yes*' (He hands it to the teacher) or
'*No — Fish*'(The teacher picks one from the centre pile).

Studying words and remembering them
A child may have some reading skill but may show little skill in accumulating new words or profiting from instruction given only the day before. It is as if he cannot 'hold' the experience, and store it for future use.

Develop a way of studying words
Help the child to develop a consistent approach to remembering words. Adapt it to suit the strengths and weaknesses of each child.

• Ask the child to look at the word written on the blackboard or with magnetic letters or in large print. Say it slowly and run your finger across it.
• Ask him to do this.
• Ask him to close his eyes and see it, saying it in parts.
• Ask him to look again, scanning it without help, and saying it in parts. (The problem is probably that he does not search with his eyes the letter outlines, or the letter sequences.)
• Ask him to write it, or parts of it, without looking. (Do not be too strict on this point for young children.) Have him say it as he writes it.

Now present the words in different ways calling for the same responses from the child.

Practise word reconstruction
• Make the word out of magnetic letters. Jumble and remake until the child is fluent.
• Write the word on the blackboard in large print using verbal instructions while writing each letter.

Introduce tracing
If visual analysis and word reconstruction do not produce good results, introduce tracing and add the feel of the movements to the child's sources of information.

• Ask the child to trace the word with finger contact saying the part of the word as he traces it. *Finger contact is important.*
• Repeat this process as often as is necessary until the child can write the word without looking at the copy.
• Write the word on scrap paper as often as is needed to reach fluency.

Other activities
• Encourage the child to include the word in his written story.
• Choose books that include the new word.
• Establish fluency in producing this vocabulary of known words.

A way of remembering
When a child has used these rather laborious strategies for establishing his early visual memories for a small vocabulary of words he usually arrives at the stage where he can take short cuts.

'. . . one of the most interesting things to be found in our non-reading cases (was that) the child, who had to trace each word many times at first, eventually developed the ability to glance over the words of four and five syllables, say them once or twice as he looked at them and then write them without a copy.'

(Fernald, 1943, pp. 21ff)

The child is then able to learn from the printed word by merely looking at it and saying it to himself before he writes it. He may use one of several strategies — silent articulation, visual scanning or some other aid.

Dale was certain about his visual memory for some words. The teacher said, '*Have a look at "come", a really good look and then write it down there.*'

Dale replied, '*I don't have to look.*' He covered his eyes and wrote the word. But his final comment was interesting. He said, '*Then you aren't looking and your eyes help you.*'

Relating new words to old

If something is completely novel it requires a great deal of effort to learn about it. If we can relate the new item to something we already know it is easier to master.

To make the child an independent reader the teacher must encourage him to search for links between new words and words he already knows.

Word construction, demolition and substitution activities help to build such habits of search.

Questioning during book reading can also foster a search for relationships.

16 Children Who Are Hard To Accelerate

Introduction

The patterns of progress made by children will be very different from child to child. For hundreds of children in New Zealand Reading Recovery Programme acceleration is the outcome of sound teaching. As the child gains control of the various components of the reading process the teacher who is observing sensitively begins to realise that a faster pace up through text difficulty levels is possible. (See page 52.) However, for some children and some teachers this does not seem to happen.

There is only one position to take in this case. The programme is not, or has not been, appropriately adapted to the child's needs. It is time to take a close look at possible reasons for this, and colleague comment is what the teacher should seek.

Steps to take

1 First check up on yourself as teacher.

• Have you made some assumptions about the child that could be wrong?
• Are you operating the programme as required?
• Is your programme addressing the child's strengths and weaknesses that were revealed in the Diagnostic Survey?
• Is writing receiving attention? Or *enough* attention?
• Have you taught in such a way that the child has learned to depend on you, and not to take the initiative?

2 Now check up on your records of the child's progress.

• Look at the first Diagnostic Survey, particularly at the low scores. Which parts of the programme would be difficult because of these?
• Look over your Lesson Plans and describe what the succession of learning/failing to learn has been in particular areas. What have your records to say about the things that this child has found difficult?

3 Now set about observing the child's behaviour very closely.

• Ask yourself questions about why he might be finding parts of the task difficult.

Take stock of what you have found in these three areas. Re-read the appropriate parts of your supporting texts, using the index.

Then talk out your problems with some Reading Recovery colleagues.

• You may decide that you have to work out some new ways of getting the child to do the 'reading work' in the areas in which he is opting out. Use all your ingenuity. Ask others to watch you and the child at work and check out what is happening.

In general, when the child is hard to accelerate there is some part or parts of the reading process that he finds difficult. Often he has learned to do something which is interfering with his progress, and he may have learned it from the way you have been teaching.

Another reason for the child finding it hard is that some important aspect of the reading process has not received attention. It has been left out rather than learned in an interfering way.

For most children, whatever the problem, it is wise to drop the level of text difficulty, as a first step. This seems in conflict with the aim to accelerate the child. However, it is the *child* who accelerates, and in one sense the teacher merely matches the texts to the child's rate of acceleration. So, starting on easier text, the child will need to orchestrate the whole process in a more satisfactory way, before moving off up the difficulty sequence.

The things to check suggested above were:

• your own teaching behaviour
• your analysis of the child's difficulties
• new explanations that might apply
• the intactness of the reading process on easier material
• whether the child's writing behaviour is improving.

You are likely to have some blind spots in these areas and the opinions of colleagues could be most useful for the readjustment of your programme. It has been one of the values of the Inservice Training sessions that teachers have been able to pool their collective wisdom on their most puzzling pupils.

9 When to Discontinue Children

Transfer Out Of The Programme

This decision must be weighed up very carefully.

Part of the intensive programme in Reading Recovery is the close supervision by the teacher. This is not typical of the usual classroom programme because of the number of children who need attention.

Early in the Reading Recovery programme the teacher must begin to prepare the child for this transfer. She must never do for the child what he could do for himself. She encourages and reinforces independent operating, and problem detection, and problem-solving. Her teaching must defeat a common outcome of remedial programmes which is that they make the pupils dependent on the teacher. Reading Recovery aims to make children independent of the teacher.

Back in the classroom it would be ideal if the child could work on his own, and be confident enough to know when to appeal for help and how to use that help. He needs to be able to continue to increase his control over reading and writing even with a 'not-noticing' teacher.

For these reasons decisions to discontinue should be made very carefully.

Deciding when to discontinue

How can we decide whether a child is ready for discontinuing the individual tutoring? There can be no hard and fast criteria because the aim will be to replace a child in a class group in which he can continue to make progress, and this will differ from child to child and from school to school.

Consultation will be necessary — with the class teacher, and the teacher in charge of the Junior School. Recorded observations of the child's behaviour during a class reading lesson will give important information for decisions about continuing or discontinuing tuition.

Reading Recovery teachers found these questions helped them to decide whether a child was ready to be discontinued. (See Record Sheet p.130.)

Setting

Is there an appropriate group at his level towards the middle of his present class? Think about the size of the group, the book level at which they are working, their rate of progress, and the teacher's attitude. The child should enter the group at a somewhat lower level than he was working on with his Reading Recovery teacher.

Survival

How well will this child survive back in his class? Will he continue to learn from his own efforts? Has he acquired some of the strategies in a self-improving system? What evidence do you have from his reading? Or from his writing?

Running record analysis

Does he read increasingly difficult material always at 90 percent accuracy or above? Does he read (easy) books for pleasure?

Estimate of scores

Do you expect his scores to have improved on the tasks of the survey? What evidence do you have to support this? Where was he weak before? Will he be able to score much higher now?

Observable behaviours to look for at discontinuing

There is no fixed set of strategies nor any required levels of text nor any test score that must be attained to warrant discontinuing. It is essential that the child has a system of strategies which work in such a way that the child learns from his own attempts to read. Some of the things a child ready for discontinuing will be able to do will be these.

- *Directional movement*. The child will have control over this without lapses, or else will be aware of his tendency to lapse and will be able to check on his own behaviour.
- *One to one matching*. The child can adopt a controlled one to one matching of spoken to written words for checking purposes.
- *Self-monitoring*. The child is checking on himself. This can be seen when an error is noticed but not corrected. It is also observed as the child reassembles a cut-up story.
- *Cross-checking*. The child notices discrepancies in his own responses by cross-checking one kind of cue (say, visual) with a different kind of cue (such as meaning).
- *Use of multiple cue sources*. On self-correction behaviour it is sometimes clear that the child is using meaning, and structure, and visual cues and a sense of how words are written, trying to achieve a match across all sources of cues.
- *Self-correction*. Effective self-correction follows from using self-monitoring, searching for cues, and cross-checking cues. However attempts at self-correction though unsuccessful are also indicators that the child is aware these activities can be helpful.

Questions of level

Usually the child ready for discontinuing can read a text which the average child in his second year at school can read. He can write a couple of sentences for his story requiring only one or two words from the teacher. Check the record of words written independently and the stories he writes, and make sure there has been marked improvement, and that a strategy of getting from sounds to letters has developed.

If discontinuing —

As the next step in discontinuing prepare the child and his class teacher for this, perhaps working with the child in his classroom for the last two weeks of his programme.

Then *test the child* on the Diagnostic Survey and analyse the strengths and weaknesses at this point in time. Compare them with the earlier testing and note the areas in which progress occurred. At this point decide finally to discontinue.

Discuss the child's current status with his class teacher.

Offer to monitor the child's progress, say once every two weeks or once a month, until you and his teacher are sure that he is continuing to make progress.

If not discontinuing —

The teacher may make a decision like one of the following:

- The child needs to continue in the full programme.
- The child needs further help in two or three areas where he is still weak; i.e. text reading, hearing sounds in sequence, word analysis, etc.
- The child needs further help to survive in the class situation.

- The child needs one or two individual text reading sessions each week for motivation, as a check, to gain confidence, or any other reasons.

Set new learning goals. Aim to make the child independent. Continue only as long as necessary. Make new plans for discontinuing, testing only in the critical areas on this occasion.

Follow-up and check-up

Research studies which followed children who had remedial instruction have often reported that progress was not maintained back in the classroom. Research following up Reading Recovery children (see pp 91-95, 100-104) showed that, in general, progress was sustained for most of the children. However, some children made slow progress for a year and then accelerated again while other children began to lag in progress after two years.

The numbers of such children were small but they led us to recommend that Reading Recovery teachers or some other person given this role, should:

- monitor progress sensitively in the next three years
- consider promotions carefully (and not overpromote)
- provide further individual help if needed particularly if progress slows.

Although Reading Recovery children perform well in their classes some of them remain at-risk children, easily thrown by life circumstances or poor learning experiences. A refresher course of individual instruction for quite a short period should be most helpful for a 'recovered' child who has begun to slip behind his classmates.

10 The Reading Recovery Research Reports

A research programme was undertaken to explore the extent to which it was possible to undercut reading failure by a programme of early intervention. The research programme consisted of six projects.

1 The Development Project, 1976-77
2 The Field Trial Research in 1978
3 The One Year Follow-up Research, 1979
4 The Replication Study, 1979
5 The Analysis of Lesson Content, 1978
6 The Three Year Follow-up, 1981
7 Summary

1 The Development Project, 1976-77

The aim of the project was to record how teachers worked with children having marked difficulty learning to read, in a one to one teaching situation. We aimed to describe the range and variability of reading behaviours shown by the children and the range and variability of the teaching responses made by the teachers. The children had just completed their first year at school.

The project began with practitioners, a team of six people — teachers, supervising teachers, reading advisers and senior University students. They agreed to find time to teach two children individually. They agreed to meet once every two weeks to observe each other teach and to discuss procedures and assumptions. Procedures were evolved for observing the teachers at work, using a one way screen. At these sessions, the team would discuss pupil and teacher responses as they occurred and following the lesson they would challenge the teachers who had demonstrated to explain why they chose a technique, a particular book or a specific progression. They were asked:

• what contributed to a teaching decision?
• how could they justify it?
• what other difficulties or achievements were the procedures related to?
• why did the children react in this or that way?
• why did they not move the child more quickly?

During such discussions the implicit assumptions of the teacher had to be explained verbally rather than remaining intuitive hunches. The process of articulating the basis for a teaching decision was always difficult.

A large number of techniques were piloted, observed, discussed, argued over, related to theory, analysed, written up, modified and tried out in various ways, and, most important, many were discarded. Carefully graded sequences within each technique were described. Thus the procedures were derived from the responses of experienced teachers to children as they tried to read and write. The process of refinement continued over the next three years, as several drafts of the teaching procedures were written, discussed and edited by the teachers. The procedures were derived from the practice of teachers who were working with failing children but they were discussed and analysed in relation to current theories of the reading process.

The six-year-old children who were referred to the programme were diverse in their response to print. No two children had quite the same problems. Children on the same level of text varied in their profiles of test scores. One may conclude therefore that these children read texts of similar difficulty with skills of different strengths. It follows from this that each child's reading recovery programme must be designed to suit the skills in his repertoire and so programmes differed from child to child.

Critical evaluation of the results of the development project suggested that the five most important areas to receive attention in the next stage of our project would be these.

1 *Organisation*. Children probably needed more intensive programmes than two or three lessons each week.

2 *Teaching*. The most effective teaching procedures from our pooled resources should be gathered together and articulated to provide better guidance for teachers.

3 *Efficient Choices*. If effective teaching is to occur sound choices must be made about appropriate procedures. It follows that certain procedures are de-emphasised or eliminated from some children's programmes. Decisions not to do certain things in recovery programmes may be very important. This is a somewhat novel concept in the area of reading difficulties. It relates to economical use of the child's learning time.

4 *Conceptualising the goal*. The goal of teaching should be a self-improving system, a set of behaviours which lead the child to control more difficult texts merely because he reads them. The important components of a self-improving system are the in-the-head strategies which the child initiates to detect that an error has been

made and to find some way of righting the wrong, or to find some way of using past knowledge to solve a novel problem. Teachers in our next phase would need to deliberately focus the child's attention on such operations.

5 *Transfer or generalisation*. We must think clearly about the process of discontinuing children from tutoring and the ways in which we could ensure continuing progress back in classrooms. If it is not a contradiction of concepts we must be specific about such generalisation.

2 The Field Trial Research in 1978

We had observed good teachers of problem readers working in one to one situations, and we had observed the children. Gradually we had articulated what we thought were some of the children's problems, and what seemed to be efficient, helpful and economical teaching procedures.

The next step was to demonstrate that these procedures worked and that children made progress. However if an early intervention programme were to be adopted in schools we also had to demonstrate that our procedures could work in different school settings. Such evidence would be most important for New Zealand educators who are traditionally very sceptical about the contribution that academics and researchers can make to effective teaching. In addition we would somehow have to find convincing evidence to support the argument for one-to-one teaching, for which there was no precedent in the system.

The research questions

The practical questions concerned how the programme could be implemented in schools.

• Could teachers without specialist training or university study use the procedures effectively?
• How would the programmes need to vary from school to school?

The plan of operation must allow for teachers to differ, for schools to differ, and the children in different schools to differ. How teachers worked, how many children they took each day or week, and what timetables they derived were not predetermined. Teachers discussed their ideas on these matters with the research staff. Consultation, not prescription was the key word. We wanted to see what organisation teachers would evolve for mounting the programme in their schools.

The other questions concerned what reading progress could be made.

• To what extent could the poorest readers be helped by individual tutoring?
• How many could be helped?
• What were the outcomes of the programme for the tutored children in comparison with the untutored?
• Could the gains made in tutoring be sustained after withdrawal of the supplementary tutoring?

The schools

The schools were different in size, in type of organisation*, in population and location. All were in the suburbs of a large metropolitan area. School **A** was a small school in an older state housing area with some solo parents. School **B** was in a mixed working and middle class suburb. School **C** was on the edge of both a middle class and a working class new housing area and was the biggest school. In School **D** the children were predominantly from working class backgrounds with a high proportion of Maori and Pacific Island children and much movement in and out of the school. School **E** was a larger school in a newer state housing area with 60 percent of the children having solo parents.

The teachers

Principals in those five schools were asked to use the allocated extra teacher to release an experienced teacher of beginning reading who volunteered to do this Reading Recovery training. The teachers released had from five to 12 years experience. Academic background was not a requirement. All the teachers had been trained in Teachers Colleges and did not have University Diplomas or degrees. The conditions of a school's participation in the research study were:

• that the teacher be allowed to test *every 6-year-old* within two weeks of his/her birthday
• that she arrange a programme of individual tutoring for suitable children
• that her participation in this programme would not be interrupted for any reason (such as relieving, sports duties and school trips).

Testing every child after one year of instruction

To allow for comparison of the children who received help with their classmates who did not, the total age cohort was tested in the five schools. The dates of testing, linked to sixth birthdays were scattered throughout the year for children whose birthdays fell between 1 September, 1977

*Two were open-plan and three had single-cell classrooms.

and 30 September, 1978. The mean age of the 291 children at initial testing was six years 1.5 months because testing which began in February 1978 included children born in the previous September. Children who transferred into the schools later in the year were tested if they belonged to the same age cohort.

Who was tutored?

From the 291 children in the age cohort in five schools 122 were given special help.

How children were distributed on the reading books after one year of school differed markedly from school to school. Two main reasons for this were that the children entering schools differed in background experience and ability from school to school and that schools paced the introduction of the reading programme differently. Some schools began book reading early and pushed ahead rather rapidly. Others took a longer time to establish foundation skills. Therefore children selected for individual tutoring were not chosen by setting a particular attainment level. *They were the lowest scorers on text reading in that particular school.* The lowest scorers in School **C** might be better than some of the higher scorers in School **E**. It was not the point of this study to raise all children's performance above a particular level. A teacher was available in each school and she was trying to raise the performance of the low progress readers *in that school.*

The working week of the teacher set limits on how many children were in her programme. The responsiveness of children to individual teaching determined the weeks a child remained in the study. Factors which tended to lengthen time in the programme were language problems, family mobility, unsettled family circumstances, sickness and/or absence, general retardation, and unusual learning problems.

The proportion of the age-cohort who were individually tutored differed from school to school because of the school's size and because of the variations in the needs of the children.

The tutoring programme

Children received individual daily teaching by selected teachers who were undergoing a year's inservice training. Training sessions were held every two weeks. This allowed a continuing quality control over the teaching on the one hand, but, on the other hand, the teachers were apprentices, learning how to implement the programme and coming to grips with the decision-making it called for.

The teacher who had completed a Diagnostic Survey Report had on hand an analysis of behaviours which should relate directly to her teaching programme.

A typical teaching session included a particular set of activities (see pp 59-81). These placed the emphasis on using text for most of the lession. As the goal of the programme was to return children to average reading groups in their classrooms it was necessary to accelerate their progress to achieve this. Accelerated progress would be most likely to be achieved if:

- the child had many opportunities to practise
- the task was the same as the one on which improvement was required, i.e. reading messages written in sentences
- the child was building a complex, flexible system of alternative responses (Clay, 1979).

If skills are taught in isolation more time must be spent in learning to combine these, and more difficulty is experienced with switching to alternative responses.

The teacher arranged to see children on a timetable that suited her and the school. Sometimes this was once a day and sometimes twice a day for two sessions (see Table 1). Occasionally towards the end of their programme children would come to her in twos and threes but most of the teaching was done in an individual programme which supplemented the work of the classroom.

The teacher training

The teachers were being trained throughout the year. Teachers were encouraged to draw on their experience at first. Gradually Reading Recovery procedures were introduced and demonstrated, and teachers were encouraged to change their concept of the task. Every two weeks one of the five teachers would demonstrate by teaching one of her pupils while the other teachers observed and discussed the procedures on the other side of a one-way screen.

Topics raised by the teachers in these discussions seemed to suggest that their attention to the reading process was shifting:

- from teaching for items of knowledge (letters known, words remembered) and getting the child to habituate a skill or memorise a new element,
- to developing in the child the confidence and willingness to use a variety of text-solving strategies.

Another feature of the shift was away from having the 'poor reader' dependent on the teacher and towards teaching in such a way that the child had many opportunities to teach himself something.

Records

Teachers were encouraged to keep a diary or log book as a personal history of the year's work. Personal reactions and queries were to be dated and entered on both teacher behaviours and perceptions, and child behaviours. In addition each teacher kept these records on individual pupils.

- A Diagnostic Summary Report was prepared for each child when he was accepted into the project.
- A Lesson Plan or a Lesson Summary was kept for each session with the child, detailing at what point in the teaching sequence the teacher was working and how the child responded. This provided a record of the small step gains made by each child, and of the progressions which the teacher selected from the teachers' handbook or manual.
- One Running Record of text reading was usually kept for each session.
- A graph of progress by Book Level was plotted from one Running Record each week.

Contact with parents

We hoped schools would feel free to approach parents in whatever would be their normal procedure. In fact, contacts during this first year were minimal.

The discontinuing of tutoring

When the teachers judged from the children's work that they would be able to work with and survive in an appropriate group in their classroom and maintain their progress they recommended the child for discontinuing.

At this point an independent tester re-administered the Diagnostic Survey to provide an objective check on the teacher's estimate of progress. In most cases when a comparison was made with the entry test scores, progress in all tests and on text reading was noted and individual tutoring was discontinued. Sometimes a recommendation was made to continue intermittent lessons to support a child or give further instruction in specific areas of weakness. Occasionally a child was not ready to be discontinued. In most cases the teachers had carried the children for longer and to higher levels than we had expected. They were conservative in their recommendations for discontinuing.

New children entered individual tutoring as others were discontinued.

Testing at the end of 1978

In the last two months of 1978 all children were re-tested by two independent testers.

Book Level and Reading Vocabulary were two measures of reading progress used.

1   Book Level (Running Records)

The most relevant measure for demonstrating progress was Book Level because it assessed the child's management of cues arising in sequences in a text. A scale of difficulty was provided by two Caption Book steps, 24 steps for the basic reading series* plus three paragraphs

*The New Zealand Ready to Read series, (1963).

(2, 3 and 4) from the Neale Analysis of Reading Ability, making 29 steps. The highest level on the scale that a child could attempt with 90 percent (or above) accuracy determined his score. This type of measure had proved to be a valid and reliable test of reading progress in other research (Clay, 1966; Robinson, 1973; Wade, 1978). It is not an equal interval scale.

2   Reading Vocabulary

A standardised test was also used. Previous research with children of this age in New Zealand schools (Clay, 1966) had shown that low progress children could be given the Word Test and high progress children could be given the Schonell R1 test and that a satisfactory measure *for research purposes* was obtained by combining these two scores. This procedure was used again in this study and the combined scores for Reading Vocabulary yielded a normal distribution. A Word Test score provides only a sign or indicator of reading progress, because the test behaviour that is scored does not involve management of the behaviours needed to read continuous text.

The other tests used were from the Diagnostic Survey: Concepts About Print (CAP), Letter Identification (LI), Writing Vocabulary (WV), Dictation Test (DIC), (Clay, 1979).

Scores on these tests were interpreted as indicators of some component reading skills covering directional and visual discrimination learning (CAP), letter identity (LI), words known in every detail (WV) and sound-to-letter association (DIC).

Results: organisational factors

How did teachers adapt this opportunity for individual instruction to the setting of their particular school?

Numbers and sex of children

The number of children who received tuition from teachers ranged from 20 to 30 per teacher per year working fulltime (Table 1). 61 percent of the children tutored were boys and 39 percent were girls.

Weeks in programme

Table 1 shows the average pattern, and individual school averages, for time in tuition. There was an average lag of three to five weeks between sixth birthday and entry to the programme, for a variety of unavoidable reasons such as vacations, a full tutoring roll, a need for testing to be scheduled and/or absences.

The average length of individual programmes was 13 to 14 weeks. It should be stressed that this was an *average* length of time in tuition; individual children needed more time in the programme.

Organisation Differences in Five Schools

	Number of children in tuition	Mean Weeks in Programme		Mean length of lessons (in minutes)	Mean number of lessons
		Discontinued	Not Discontinued		
A[1]	22	15.1	12.0	40.5	27.6
B[2]	28	11.3	11.8	40.0	21.8
C	22	11.6	13.0	35.9	33.8
D	29	13.2	13.8	26.7[3]	33.3
E[1], E[2]	21	16.2	15.1	40.0	26.4
Average		14.0	13.1		

Table 1

[1]   These schools had women principals, the others had men.

[2]   These schools had open plan or open space organisation for junior classes.

[3]   Mean length of lesson was affected by some use of group instruction.

Length of lessons

The arrangements that teachers made for lessons varied from child to child and from teacher to teacher. Three teachers used a 40 minute lesson most of the time and others used a short and a long lesson, one of 30 minutes and a second of 10 minutes later in the day (Table 1).

Results: progress of the children

The progress of three groups will be reported.

Control Group. The 160 children not selected for tutoring (who were of the same age group, attended the same schools and had higher initial attainment), were used as a reference group for the tutored children.

Discontinued. Children who were tutored and discontinued during the school year had been back in the class programme for an average of 12 weeks (N = 53). Another discontinued group were those who were receiving tuition up until the time of final testing and who met the criteria used to discontinue children (N = 27). These two subgroups make up the Discontinued group.

Not Discontinued. These were children who were receiving tuition at the time of final testing and who needed further instruction (N = 42).

Within-group changes

The mean test scores of all three groups (Discontinued/Not Discontinued and Control) increased from initial to final testing on Book Level, Reading Vocabulary, Concepts About Print, Dictation, and Letter Identification so that statistically-significant differences were recorded (see Table 2). Writing Vocabulary was not administered initially to the Control group, but significant differences were found for both tutored groups.

Figure 1 shows the progress of the three groups on Book Level at initial and final testing. The Reading Vocabulary Test graph (not shown) plotted a similar shift. Despite the very different nature of these measures, one measuring accuracy on text and the other word reading in isolation, the type of change for each group was similar.

Initial and Final Test — Scores

Test	Group	Test Time	N	Mean	SD	Sm	t test[1] of differences	Correlation of initial and final test
Book Level	Discontinued	1	80	6.33	3.67	0.41	25.80	0.53*
		2	80	18.53	3.96	0.44		
	Not Discontinued	1	42	2.48	1.61	0.25	15.12	0.48*
		2	42	8.21	2.76	0.43		
	Control	1	160	12.54	5.86	0.46	22.12	0.64*
		2	160	20.86	5.47	0.43		
Reading Vocabulary	Discontinued	1	80	9.25	9.32	1.04	4.09	0.42*
		2	80	27.63	6.46	0.72		
	Not Discontinued	1	42	4.76	2.96*	0.46	12.28	0.47*
		2	42	14.76	5.20	0.80		
	Control	1	160	24.03	16.78	1.33	19.18	0.74*
		2	160	33.53	11.51	0.91		
Concepts About Print	Discontinued	1	80	13.86	2.78	0.31	18.14	0.35*
		2	80	19.79	2.34	0.26		
	Not Discontinued	1	42	10.90	2.89	0.45	16.05	0.71*
		2	42	16.00	2.45	0.38		
	Control	1	160	16.83	3.43	0.27	5.73	0.64*
		2	160	17.41	3.77	0.30		
Letter Identification	Discontinued	1	80	37.20	13.52	1.51	9.92	0.14
		2	80	51.55	3.20	0.36		
	Not Discontinued	1	42	23.67	14.39	2.22	12.78	0.72*
		2	42	43.29	9.59	1.48		
	Control	1	160	49.86	8.67	0.69	3.91	0.55*
		2	160	50.74	6.30	0.50		
Writing Vocabulary	Discontinued	1	80	10.38	5.80	0.65	17.67	0.18
		2	80	45.69	12.24	1.59		
	Not Discontinued	1	42	5.64	2.90	0.45	14.92	0.47*
		2	42	24.05	9.21	1.42		
	Control	1		(Not administered)				
		2	160	48.19	21.76	1.72		
Dictation	Discontinued	1	80	15.44	7.83	0.88	21.39	0.31*
		2	80	33.24	2.97	0.33		
	Not Discontinued	1	42	8.29	7.31	1.13	17.31	0.62*
		2	42	24.52	6.53	1.01		
	Control	1	160	27.70	8.59	0.68	6.50	0.65*
		2	160	32.96	5.82	0.46		

1 All t-tests are above 2.69 and are significant.
* Correlations that were significantly above zero at the p<.01 level have an asterisk.

Table 2

Gain Scores for all Measures						
(with t-tests for significant differences between groups)						
Test	Group	N	Mean	SD	SE$_m$	t
Book Level	Discontinued	80	2.84	1.13	0.13	4.62*
	Not Discontinued	42	2.00	0.80	0.22	
	Control	160	2.06	1.20	1.11	0.29
Reading Vocabulary	Discontinued	80	2.76	1.01	0.11	5.30*
	Not Discontinued	42	1.69	0.87	0.13	
	Control	160	1.89	1.23	0.11	0.94
Concepts About Print	Discontinued	80	2.99	1.51	0.17	9.65*
	Not Discontinued	42	2.14	1.00	0.15	
	Control	160	1.19	1.14	0.13	4.83*
Letter Identification	Discontinued	80	2.33	1.36	0.15	5.47*
	Not Discontinued	42	1.83	0.93	0.14	
	Control	160	1.34	1.17	0.11	2.45
Writing Vocabulary	Discontinued	80	4.15	1.28	0.14	9.06*
	Not Discontinued	42	2.00	1.17	0.18	
	Control	(Not administered)				
Dictation	Discontinued	80	2.71	1.14	0.13	8.29*
	Not Discontinued	42	2.14	0.95	0.15	
	Control	160	1.38	1.11	0.10	3.99*

* t-test indicates a significant difference between groups.

Table 3

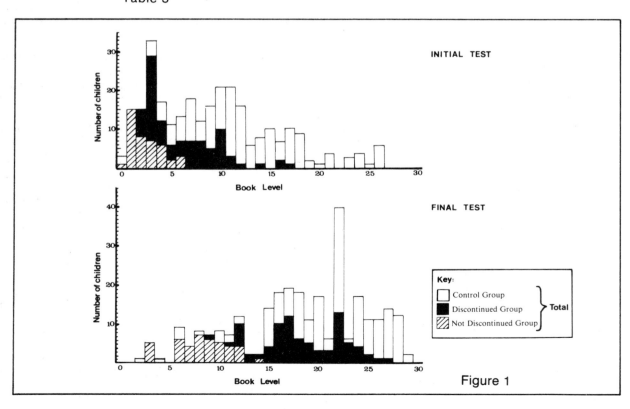

Figure 1

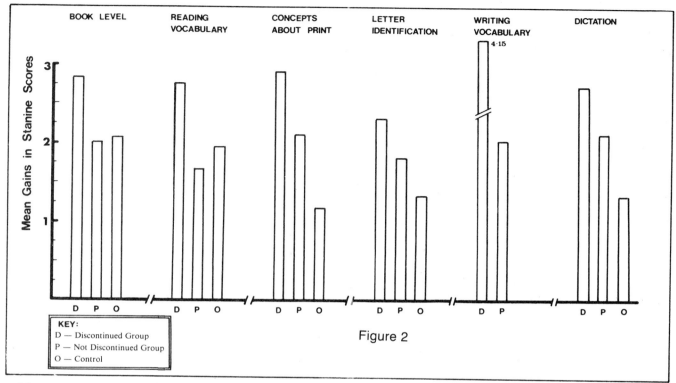

Figure 2

The movement of the Discontinued group from low level scoring to average levels is visually apparent and the fact that the Not Discontinued group need further tuition can also be noted.

A third way of reporting the progress was with the gains in Stanine scores. These are reported in Table 3 and Figure 2.

The pupils who received individual tuition made gains which equalled or exceeded the gain scores made by their classmates who showed initially the higher achievement. The following statements refer to the number of Stanines *gained* but they do not imply that the groups were scoring at the same level on the tests.

a   The Discontinued group made higher and significantly different gains from the Control group in all tests. (Writing Vocabulary was not administered initially to the Control group.) (Table 3 and Figure 2.)

b   The Not Discontinued group made gains that were not significantly lower than those of the Control group on Book Level, Reading Vocabulary and Letter Identification. They were significantly higher on Concepts About Print and Dictation.

c   The Discontinued group made significantly higher gains than the Not Discontinued pupils on Writing Vocabulary.

The only children in the age cohort (282) for whom the programme was insufficient or unsuitable, were:

• four Pacific Island children with insufficient English to understand the instructions of the Diagnostic Survey (and presumably the instructional programmes). Many Pacific Island children made satisfactory progress in the programme,
• one Indian child with flaccid cerebral palsy who made little progress and who was referred to the Psychological Service,
• two children who were helped in the programme but were also seen by the Psychological Service as possibly needing placement in special classes for children of low intelligence.

Further comment on the Field Trial phase has been made in the one-year follow-up research (next section).

3 The One-Year Follow-Up Study, 1979

One year later the progress of all these children was re-assessed. Many things could have upset any trends established by tutoring in the previous year. Control children might forge ahead at a faster rate once the early skills had been mastered as they profitted from wide-ranging individual reading. Discontinued children might be unable to build on their gains and so slip back. Not Discontinued children might have slipped further behind or they might have been able to accelerate their progress. No further individual help had been provided during this year.

The research questions

Questions for the one year follow-up study were:

- what gains were made in 1979?
- was the relative status of the groups maintained?
- were gains made during tutoring sufficient to allow children to progress with their average classmates?
- were the gains made better than those predicted by the statistical phenomena of regression to the mean?

The research phases

This description of phases is necessary for the interpretation of the tables and figures in this section.

The children entered school on their fifth birthdays and were tested one year later, on their sixth birthdays. As this birthday occurred anywhere between September 1977 and September 1978 the first phase began for individual children at variable dates throughout the year.

The Tutoring Phase (Phase 1)   The tutoring phase began soon after a child's sixth birthday and continued as long as necessary to meet preset criteria of performance based on reading strategies. On average a period of 13-14 weeks was needed. Children were discharged from tutoring when they demonstrated a set of behaviours thought to be related to surviving in the ordinary classroom programme. If children did not demonstrate these behaviours they continued in the programme. Of necessity the tutoring phase ended for all children at the end of the school year, December 1978.

Back-in-class Phase (Phase 2)   The decisions about discontinuing tutoring and the staggered timing of the children's entry into the tutoring phase created a group of children who had a period back in their classroom after tutoring and before the end of the school year.

The Follow-up Phase (Phase 3)   No contact was made with the children during 1979. Some moved to new schools. In December, 1979, all children who could be located in the Auckland area were retested. Of the 291 children originally tested in five schools at six years 282 were retested in December, 1978, (97%) and 270 in December, 1979 (93%). Numbers in the groups at follow-up were Control 153 (160), Discontinued 76 (80), Not Discontinued 41 (42). The losses were low in number and spread across the group.

Results

Table 4 and Figures 3 and 4 summarise the comparisons at Initial, Final and Follow-up testing for the total group and each subgroup. Mean scores rose during Reading Recovery instruction for tutored groups and gains continued in the following year at a satisfactory level.

		Mean			SD		
Test	Group	6:0	1978	1979 (end of)	6:0	1978	1979 (end of)
Book Level	Total	9.40	18.51	24.39	6.22	6.42	4.92
	Control	12.54	20.86	26.36 ⎤	5.86	5.47	3.29
	Discontinued	6.33	18.53	24.66 ⎬ *	3.67	3.96	3.10
	Not Discontinued	2.48	8.21	16.23 ⎦ *	1.61	2.76	4.75
Reading Vocabulary	Total	16.20	28.86	41.52	10.40	11.29	13.13
	Control	24.03	33.53	47.07 ⎤	16.78	11.51	12.11
	Discontinued	9.25	27.63	39.09 ⎬ *	9.32	6.46	7.36
	Not Discontinued	4.76	14.76	24.59 ⎦ *	2.96	5.20	8.99

Mean Scores for Research Groups on Book Level and Reading Vocabulary

Table 4   * Differences are significant at p <.01 level.

Mean scores for READING VOCABULARY at Initial, Discontinuing, Final and Follow-Up testing for Control, Discontinued and Not Discontinued groups.

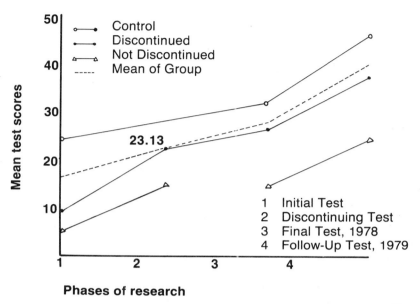

Reading Vocabulary

Figure 3

Mean scores for BOOK LEVEL at Initial, Discontinuing, Final and Follow-Up testing for Control, Discontinued and Not Discontinued group

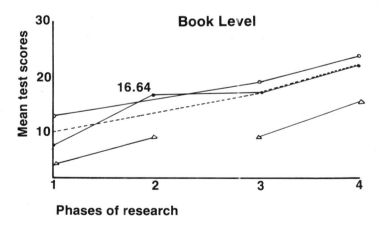

Book Level

Figure 4

The Control group scored above the mean of the total group at each of three testing times (Initial, Final and Follow-Up) on two test variables, Book Level and Reading Vocabulary.

The Discontinued group of children had low Initial scores. Final scores were well within one standard deviation of the Control group's Final means, and they retained that position at Follow-Up testing. It would be reasonable to claim that children in that position should be able to profit from the usual classroom instruction. This applied to both the Book Level and Reading Vocabulary measures.

	Correlations between Initial Scores And Final Scores (3-11 months) And Follow-Up Scores (15-23 months)				
	Time	Control	Discontinued	Not Discontinued	Total
Book Level	Final	.64	.54	.48	
	Follow-Up	.50	.30	.48	.61
Reading Vocabulary	Final	.74	.42	.47	
	Follow-Up	.63	.20	.50	.71
Table 5					

For the Discontinued group the correlations of Initial scores with Final and Follow-Up scores were lower, as one would predict following this intervention programme (0.54, 0.30, 0.42, 0.20, Table 5).

For the Not Discontinued group the correlations of Initial scores with Final and Follow-Up scores were higher than for the Discontinued group (they were not so influenced by the programme) but lower than those of the Control group (0.48, 0.48, 0.47, 0.50, Table 5).

Do Initial Scores Predict Final and Follow-Up Scores?

To answer this question steps were taken that would take account of a regression to the mean effect. Pupils who score lowest tend to make the greatest gains on a second testing. It was necessary to show that any movement of the children with low reading attainment towards the mean of the group was greater than would be predicted by a regression effect. The correlation between two sets of scores for the total group was used to establish a predicted Final, and a predicted Follow-Up score for each value in the scale of scores. For every child a difference score was calculated between **a** the predicted Final and the actual Final score and **b** the predicted Follow-Up and the actual Follow-Up score. Mean difference scores for Control, Discontinued and Not Discontinued groups were compared by t-tests.

The results show that in Table 6 for Book Level and Reading Vocabulary the Control group were close to predicted scores on each variable, and on both occasions. The Discontinued children were consistently higher than would be predicted ie, their gains were greater than would be predicted by regression effects on each variable and on both occasions. The Not Discontinued children were consistently lower than would be predicted on each variable and on both occasions.

The results of the t-tests between the mean difference scores for groups show that the Discontinued group made significantly better progress than the Control group relative to their Initial scores, and this trend was maintained at Follow-Up. The Discontinued group made significantly better progress than the Not Discontinued group relative to their Initial scores and this trend was maintained at Follow-Up.

In summary, the results support the interpretation that

			Book Level		Reading Vocabulary	
Mean Difference Scores Between Predicted and Follow-Up Scores for Book Level and Reading Vocabulary**						
Group	N₁	N₂	Final	Follow-Up	Final	Follow-Up
Control	160	153	0.14	0.44	0.94	0.45
Discontinued	80	76	2.34 ⌋*	1.66 ⌋*	2.26	2.33
Not Discontinued	42	41	− 5.02 ⌋*	− 4.84 ⌋*	− 6.56 ⌋*	− 6.36 ⌋*
Table 6	*	t-tests yield significant differences at the .01 level.				
	**	A difference score of 0.00 represents no difference from the predicted score. Plus scores are higher than predicted; minus scores are lower.				

the children who were tutored until it was judged that they could survive in their classrooms were at Follow-Up one year later scoring above predicted scores while the children who were judged not to be ready for the termination of their individual tutoring programme were in every comparison below predicted scores. This is taken to be support for two theoretical arguments. The first is that the operational criteria used for judging that children were using certain processing strategies while reading were successful in separating out the two groups of children who subsequently maintained their trends of progress. The second is that the theory upon which the instructional programme was based (that gains in reading can be described in terms of operations carried out by children rather than items of knowledge gained) has received endorsement.

Supplementary Analysis 1: The Transfer Group.   During the Follow-Up Phase when no Reading Recovery programme was available to the schools 36 children of the same age cohort transferred into the research schools. They were tested at Follow-Up as a group who had not been in contact with the Reading Recovery programme. Their scores on four test variables were significantly lower than those of the total group, and lower than the Discontinued group (see Table 7) but higher than those of the Not Discontinued group. It can be argued from this that the gains of the Discontinued group were important, since they maintained a level of achievement one year later, higher than that of all children who had changed schools, a group which would include competent, average and poor achievement children.

4 Replication of the Field Trial Study, 1979 (with reduced hours of teaching)

An inservice course in 1979 guided new teachers in the operation of Reading Recovery programmes in 48 schools. These teachers worked at individual teaching for 10 hours a week, a considerable reduction on the 25 hours available in the 1978 field trial schools. Consequently the 1979 teachers taught and discontinued fewer children per teacher and lesson time was reduced from 40 to 30 minutes. Because they taught fewer children and yet selected the poorest in their schools, the children were, as a group, more challenging and difficult than those taught in the field trials.

The research question

The research question was 'Under such conditions how well would three new groups of teachers perform in comparison with the five field trial teachers in 1978?' Could the results of the first year be replicated by a large number of teachers in a large number of schools?

Procedures

The 48 schools which had teachers in training in 1979 were listed alphabetically and divided into three groups (B, C, D) providing three replication samples. The average levels of scoring for the 1979 groups (B, C, D) were compared with the 1978 field trials results (called Group A).

Results

In Table 8 and Figure 5 'Dis' refers to children discontinued with Phase 2 (see p.88), 'Dd' refers to children discontinued without Phase 2, and 'Not Dis' refers to those not ready to be discontinued.

Follow-Up Test Scores for Children who Transferred into Research Schools			
	N	Book Level	Reading Vocabulary
Control	153	26.36	47.07
Discontinued	76	24.66	39.09
Not Discontinued	41	16.44	24.59
Transfers	36	21.44	36.11
Total (without transfers)	270	24.39	41.52

Table 7

The Initial and Final scores for the four samples in Table 8 cluster within a narrow range. The samples A, B, C, D are plotted left to right in Figure 5. (See p. 97.) Results for Concepts About Print and Letter Identification tests yielded similar results. It is possible to conclude that teachers guided by a year-long inservice course were able to replicate the results of the 1978 field trials in regard to the level of most scores although they were not working full-time and therefore helped fewer children.

F-tests for each set of scores suggest the following qualifications to the above conclusion (Table 8).

Children taken into the programme in 1979 (samples B C, D) had lower scores on entry in Reading Vocabulary and Book Level but similar final scores compared with the 1978 sample. Teachers presumably retained them in the programme until they reached satisfactory levels of performance.

Final Writing Vocabulary scores tended to be lower for the 1979 groups. There is a strong possibility that teachers in 1979 with less tutoring time available gave less time to writing.

Overall the results in 1979 fairly replicated the field trials of 1978 and variations between samples were small. Time for tutoring emerged as an important variable and lower entry scores imply more individual tutoring time.

Comparison of the 1978 Sample A with Three Replication Samples in 1979 B, C, D on Initial and Final Scores

		Initial			Final		
		Dis	Dd	Not D	Dis	Dd	Not D
Reading Vocabulary	A	11.79	8.15	4.76	29.54	22.19	14.76
	B	8.39	9.53	5.85	29.98	22.42	13.73
	C	8.71	9.50	4.62	28.52	24.65	11.90
	D	8.65	6.71	4.38	28.29	23.13	12.16
	F ratios	3.87*	1.22	0.92	0.74	1.16	1.68
Book Level	A	6.94	5.07	2.48	20.17	15.04	8.21
	B	4.69	6.78	4.02	20.52	16.89	9.31
	C	5.19	7.15	2.82	19.29	17.15	8.03
	D	5.14	4.13	2.25	19.51	15.00	7.75
	F ratios	3.46*	2.91	4.67**	1.59	3.34*	1.12
Writing Vocabulary	A	11.02	9.11	5.64	51.02	39.96	24.05
	B	8.63	10.26	7.05	49.56	38.74	25.07
	C	9.08	11.55	5.15	48.10	39.10	18.77
	D	8.67	7.88	5.43	42.79	35.21	16.66
	F ratios	2.09	1.38	1.48	2.87*	0.81	4.62**
Dictation	A	16.25	13.89	8.29	34.38	31.07	24.52
	B	11.58	12.74	9.33	33.73	33.63	25.40
	C	12.65	14.90	5.61	33.63	32.85	20.72
	D	13.00	11.29	6.50	33.65	32.96	21.81
	F ratios	3.19*	0.61	2.71	0.68	2.91	2.59
Table 8		* Differences significant at .05 level.					
		** Differences significant at .01 level.					

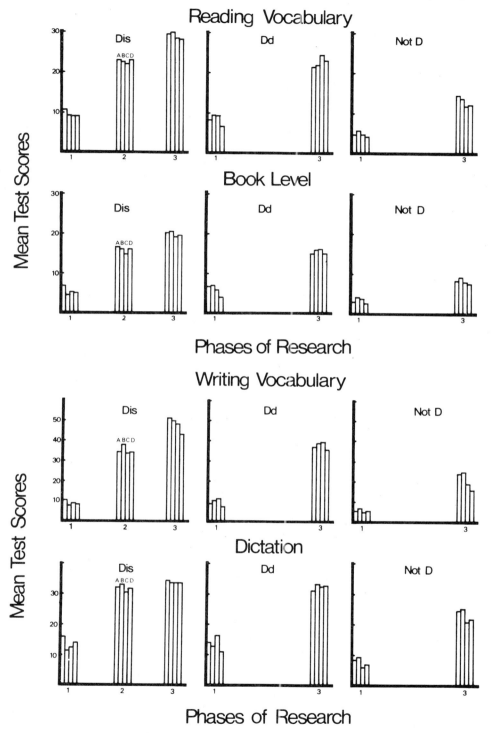

Reading Vocabulary, Book Level, Writing Vocabulary and
Dictation scores for four samples A (1978), B, C, D (1979).
Mean scores of Initial, Discontinuing and Final tests.

Figure 5

5 Programme Delivery: the Analysis of Lessons

It is important for policy-makers and researchers to know whether a programme can be delivered as designed.

In November 1981 the Department of Education approved a research grant for the retrospective analysis of the records of children who were in the Reading Recovery field trials in 1978. Teachers had been required to keep detailed notes of exactly what occurred in each individual lesson. An evaluation of the programmes delivered was made from the analysis of those records.

Finding the children

The 122 children taught during the field trials of the Reading Recovery project in 1978 were traced in December, 1981. A letter to each school brought quick returns listing the children still attending or providing the name of the next school attended. All the children were traced. Six were not available for retesting as they had left the Auckland area. This was a high retention rate after three years.

Ethnic group membership

In 1978 we did not know what ethnic groups the Reading Recovery children belonged to. In December, 1981 a research assistant visited each school to make detailed enquiries about ethnic group membership. Teaching, clerical, nursing, caretaking staff and parent helpers supplied information and the children themselves or siblings were occasionally consulted. The information included:

• all the information about the ethnic group membership of any one child, allowing for one, two or more than two group affiliations,
• the kind of evidence that informants were using to arrive at their judgements, and
• the roles of people providing the information.

Decisions were made about the quality of this information and a classification of 'Not Known' was used if these sources produced inconsistent, unreliable or insufficient information. An approach to the children's parents did not seem justified for what was a case-file re-analysis study, although we recognised that the parents would provide the most valid information.

On this information we excluded five of the 52 Maori or Pacific Island children (three children for whom we had insufficient evidence, one part-Maori child with a very high proportion of European ancestry, and one adopted child). The six children who now lived outside the Auckland District were all Polynesian, and one further child from these groups was absent from school throughout the retesting period. This reduced the available sample of Polynesian children to 40. Children who had fewer than 15 lessons were also excluded because it was decided to set a lower limit to the time spent in the programme. This resulted in the loss of a further six children reducing the number of Maori and Pacific Island children to 34, (24 Maori and 10 Pacific Island children).

The research samples

Of the 122 children who received Reading Recovery tuition in 1978, 68 were selected for the present study. No exclusions were made on the basis of achievement: the reasons for exclusion were ethnic group membership not clear (five cases), nonavailability (six cases), insufficient time in the programme (six cases), absent during testing (one case), majority group excluded by matching (36 cases). There were six samples, shown in Table 9.

Samples Used in this Study		
Polynesian Samples		**European Samples**
Maori samples		European samples
1 12 with 2 Maori parents		1 E matched to 1 on entry testing
2 12 with 1 Maori and one European parent		2 E matched to 2 on entry testing
Pacific Island sample		
3 10 with 2 parents from the same Island group		3 E matched to 3 on entry testing
Total 34		34
Table 9		

		Lesson Analysis — Reading			
Group	Sample	Lessons per week	Books Read per lesson	New Books per lesson	Books Re-read: mean accuracy
Maori	1	1.47	2.50	1.23	94.97
Maori-European	2	1.59	2.07	1.12	94.34
Pacific Island	3	1.52	2.51	1.17	95.08
European	1 E	1.59	2.16	1.21	95.57
European	2 E	1.58	2.15	1.13	95.63
European	3 E	1.96	2.06	1.22	96.47

Table 10

Results

Lesson per week

Daily lessons are a requirement in the Reading Recovery programme. The present analysis has shown that in the field trials this ideal condition was a long way from realisation. In the six subgroups the average number of lessons per week ranged from 1.47 to 1.96 (Table 10) although five per week were scheduled. Sickness, weekday holidays, absenteeism for other than health reasons and not being able to arrange for the lessons because of other school activities are the probable reasons for the low averages. They are not accounted for by teachers having to relieve in other classes or to take on other responsibilities and the school holidays were excluded from the calculations. There was a much lower rate of instruction than the programme called for, and this points to the need for Reading Recovery teachers to be active in reducing interference with daily lessons.

Average number of lessons for each group

The average number of lessons for each group ranged from 22.50 to 25.33. The lowest time was given to Pacific Island children and the highest time to Maori children. The differences are not important as the variability from child to child within the groups was very great.

Reading: Number of books per lesson

The children read between two and three books per lesson, the range for the six subgroups being 2.06 — 2.51 (Table 10). This implements the recommendations for teaching. It was suggested that the children should begin the lesson by reading one or two easy stories (books) and that later in the lesson a new book would be introduced by the teacher and then tried by the child. At least half of this reading was rereading texts previously read successfully.

Reading: New books per lesson

What was the rate at which new books were introduced? The averages ranged from 1.12 to 1.23 books per lesson (Table 10). The teachers exceeded the requirement to try to introduce a new book per lesson. The teacher was skilfully selecting books to suit the particular child's language, concept and reading development which the teacher was acutely aware of, and she was working individually with each child which meant that careful selection was possible. A new book meant a book which had not previously been worked on; it did not necessarily mean a step-up in difficulty level. Sometimes this occurred; at other times the child read at the same level of difficulty. The teachers aimed to move children as rapidly as possible through the various levels of the graded readers while allowing for two other things:

• quantities of easy reading,
• use of many different reading series and story books.

The number of new books read is consistent with these aims.

The measure of difficulty of the texts

Running records of the child's responses (correct responses, errors and self-corrections) taken on the second reading of a new book allowed for a calculation of the accuracy with which a child read a book. Teachers usually took a running record before moving the child to another book, to obtain a quantitative check on the quality of the child's reading. The mean accuracy level of the six subgroups ranged from 94.34 to 96.47, implying that the children were managing to read the texts in effective ways.

Lesson Analysis — Writing				
Group	Sample	Lessons per week	Stories per week	Stories per session
Maori	1	1.47	1.02	0.66
Maori-European	2	1.59	0.86	0.55
Pacific Island	3	1.52	1.00	0.68
European	1 E	1.59	0.99	0.66
European	2 E	1.58	1.05	0.69
European	3 E	1.96	0.96	0.56
Table 11				

Stories written

The teaching procedures required the teachers to have a story writing section in every lesson. The records show that they did not achieve this. The average number of stories written each week ranged from 0.86 to 1.05, never matching the number of lessons for any group (Table 11). The average number of stories per session ranged from 0.55 to 0.69 (Table 11).

Summary of the lesson analyses

There is a similarity across groups in the average number of sessions, the new books per lesson, the books read per lesson, and the mean accuracy levels. There is also similarity in the writing activities. At this level of analysis differences between ethnic groups in the way the programme was implemented were minimal. *Differences between the recommendations for teaching and what occurred were pronounced. The good results achieved were gained on the risky foundation of a partial implementation of the recommended programme.* Reading Recovery teachers should monitor how well they are implementing the programme so that the feedback can alert them to the areas which need closer attention.

On the basis of these data it is not possible to estimate what would happen if the recommended programme of intensive instruction were to be implemented. One might predict faster progress and a shorter intervention period. On the other hand, the shifts demanded of these children were radical compared with classroom progressions. It may be that this present rate is as fast as such children can move. No amount of guessing or argument at this stage will answer this question. Further data from a fully implemented programme would be required.

Undoubtedly, absences from school interfered with full implementation of the programme. This may indicate that, when the programme is introduced, parents need to

be consulted and a verbal contract to maximise the opportunity for the child should be entered into by both the home and school.

It may not be realistic to expect the average number of lessons to equal the number of days available for teaching but it is quite possible to make 'Stories Written' equal the number of lessons.

6   The Three Year Follow-Up Research, 1981

The research questions

Two questions were raised by educators in relation to long-term outcomes of the Reading Recovery programme.

• Were the children who had Reading Recovery programmes in 1978 continuing to progress with the average groups in their classes in December, 1981?
• Was the Reading Recovery programme suitable for Maori children?

The Reading Recovery programme undertook a difficult task. Children with the poorest performance in reading at 6:0 were selected. It was against normal expectations that such children from the low end of the achievement distribution could be brought to average levels of attainment in as little as 13-14 schools weeks in both reading and writing. Above-average levels of attainment would not be expected. It would be against normal expectations for many children to retain average placements three years later given the ups and downs of school instruction and of child health and family circumstances. With a partially implemented programme in which children who entered school in Term Three could not receive a full programme because it was only funded for a calendar year, significant results would not be predicted.

The subjects

The ethnic subgroups described in Section **5** were used (see p.98).

Results from earlier studies

Results were extracted from the studies reported in Sections **2** and **3** for these three ethnic groups. Tests of achievement were available for **a** entry to the programme, (Initial) **b** the end of the programme (Discontinuing), **c** December 1978, (Final) and **d** December 1979, (Follow-up). For some children **b** and **c** were the same time (see p.88).

The Ready to Read series of graded readers (plus some graded paragraphs from the Neale analysis [1958]) have been used in several research reports as an ordinal scale of 29 unequal steps used to indicate reading progress (see p.87). The highest level of book read at 90% accuracy or above can be used to calculate a mean book level for a group. Table 12 shows similar trends for all subgroups on mean book level with the Maori and Pacific Island groups slightly lower than the Europeans at **a**, **b**, and **c** and increasingly so at **d**.

Schonell R1, a word reading test, was used at the same testing points. Raw scores from this test are given in Table 13. The reader will note:

• the exceedingly low score of all groups at entry to the programme,

• comparable gains but low test scores at the end of the programme (Discontinuing) and at the end of 1978 because this test was unable to capture the magnitude and variety of the changes in reading behaviours that occurred at this level, and

• more or less equivalent status of the groups in December 1979 when the test provided a more reliable and valid estimate of reading level.

Mean Book Levels on Four Occasions						
Group	Sample	N	Entry	Discontinuing	End of 1978	End of 1979
			a	b	c	d
Maori	1	12	4.42	12.42	13.75	19.91
Maori-European	2	12	5.83	14.58	16.42	21.75
Pacific Island	3	10	3.00	11.50	12.50	19.90
European	1 E	12	4.58	14.58	15.92	23.83
European	2 E	12	5.75	14.92	16.92	23.18
European	3 E	10	3.90	13.20	14.20	22.60

Table 12

Schonell R1 Raw Scores on Four Occasions						
Group	Sample	N	Entry	Discontinuing	End of 1978	End of 1979
			a	b	c	d
Maori	1	12	1.75	6.58	8.50	18.45
Maori-European	2	12	2.08	7.42	10.92	20.00
Pacific Island	3	10	1.00	5.90	8.10	20.10
European	1 E	12	1.17	8.25	9.42	20.83
European	2 E	12	2.75	7.67	10.25	20.27
European	3 E	10	0.70	4.60	7.40	20.50

Table 13

Follow-Up After Three Years

Class placements

The six year olds in 1978 were about nine years old by December, 1981. They were therefore suitably placed after four years at school in either Standards Two or Three under the promotion policies of New Zealand schools. There are three educational reasons why some might be located in Standard Two.

• They had entered school in the second half of 1977 and had three or more years in the Junior classes 1-3.
• They entered school early in 1977 and being slower learners or through life circumstances (for example, illness, changes of school, family events) they required three years or more in the Junior classes 1-3.
• They were in schools where promotion rates were slower than average because of the entry characteristics of the total population of the school.

Every ex-Reading Recovery child was either in Standard Two or Three when this follow-up study was completed. Table 14 reports the number of children at or above class level for age at 1 January, 1981 for the Total group and for the sub-groups.

It is clear that schools placed the ex-Reading Recovery children according to age for class in almost all cases.

Follow-up test results

Time available between the signing of the contract for this research and the end of the school year determined the selection of tests.

• The Burt Word Reading Vocabulary Test was used because it provided 1981 norms for New Zealand children.
• The Schonell Word Reading Vocabulary Test (Schonell R1) was used because it provided a check with earlier Reading Recovery assessments (Table 13).
• Peters Word Spelling Test was used to capture control over writing vocabulary.

Text reading could not be assessed because of the time constraints.

These test results allow an evaluation to be made of one of the major claims for the Reading Recovery programme. Children are kept in the programme until they can rejoin an average group in their class and the aim has been to equip them with independent learning strategies that will enable them to maintain that position. Had this been achieved?

Class Placements By Age at 1 January, 1981: Percentages				
Age	Group	Below S2	S2	Above S2
8:0 — 8:11	Total	0	38	5
	Polynesian [1]	0	16	2
	European	0	22	3
Age	Group	Below S3	S3	Above S3
9:0 — 9:11	Total	1	24	0
	Polynesian	0	16	0
	European	1	8	0

Table 14

[1]See Table 9 page 98

Group	N	Schonell R1		Peters Spelling	
		M	SD	M	SD
Total	68	9.04	1.36	9.28	1.79
European	34	9.28	1.34	9.31	1.50
Polynesian	34	8.80	1.37	9.25	2.06

Schonell and Peters Achievement Ages for the Total Group and Ethnic Subgroups in S2 and S3 December, 1981

Table 15

Mean Achievement Ages of Each Ethnic Subgroup By Class (December, 1981)

Class	Group	N	Burt(NZ)*	Schonell R1	Peters Spelling
S2	Maori	10	7:5 — 8:0	8:1	8:5
	European	15	9:1 — 9:6	9:0	8:8
	Pacific Island	6	8:8 — 9:3	9:2	9:1
	European	7	9:5 — 10:0	9:5	9:0
S3	Maori	14	8:8 — 9:3	9:0	9:5
	European	9	10:1 — 10:6	9:7	10:1
	Pacific Island	4	10:5 — 11:0	10:0	11:0
	European	3	11:4 — 11:9	10:9	11:5

Table 16   *   The N.Z. revision of the Burt Test gives score equivalents in age bands.

Table 15 reports achievement ages for the Total group and two ethnic subgroups in December 1981 when the children were completing Standard Two or Three. Group means for reading and spelling were at expected levels for class placement. For the purpose of these analyses it has been assumed that a child in Standard Two with an achievement age of 8:0 — 9:0 years should find the class programme within his ability. The range of Standard Three was taken as 9:0 — 10:0 years. This does not take time of year into account.

Table 16 shows the mean achievement ages according to class placement for each ethnic subgroup. At the end of 1981 children were making the following progress.

• For the European and Pacific Island groups in Standard 2 (N = 28) mean test scores were within the age band for class placement.

• For the European and Pacific Island groups in Standard 3 (N = 16) mean test scores were within the age band for class placement.

• For Maori children in Standard 2 (N = 10) mean reading scores were at or below the lower limit defined as satisfactory for class level in this study but the mean spelling score was above this limit.

• For Maori children in Standard 3 (N = 14) mean reading scores were at the lower limit defined as satisfactory for class level in this study but the mean spelling score was above this level.

In an analysis which avoided the reading age bands of the Burt test by using raw scores of the Burt, Schonell and Peters tests, Maori groups had scores which were lower than Pacific Island or European children in every instance but the levels of scoring were satisfactory for class levels (Table 17).

Raw Scores on Burt, Schonell and Peters Tests For All Subgroups, December 1981 (Ages 8:0 — 9:11)								
Group	Sample	N	Burt (NZ)		Schonell R1		Peters	
			M	SD	M	SD	M	SD
Maori	1	12	46.42	17.15	33.67	13.94	28.58	11.12
Maori-European	2	12	48.00	14.24	41.42	13.99	29.27	8.95
Pacific Island	3	10	59.00	16.01	45.40	13.24	33.10	9.40
European	1 E	12	58.17	15.85	43.63	11.37	32.25	5.74
European	2 E	12	57.67	15.66	36.18	13.47	31.58	6.68
European	3 E	10	63.70	15.31	49.20	13.19	33.40	5.48
Table 17								

Lowest, Highest and Mean Scores for Subgroups (Ages 8:0 — 9:11)						
	Lowest		Mean		Highest	
Group	Maori	European	Maori	European	Maori	European
Burt (NZ)	6.1 — 6.6	7.0 — 7.5	8.1 — 8.6	9.1 — 9.6	12.3 — 12.8*	12.3 — 12.8*
Schonell R1	6.3	7.2	8.6	9.3	11.1	12.1
Peters Spelling	6.1	7.1	9.1	9.3	12.4	12.7
Ethnic Group	Pacific Is.	European	Pacific Is.	European	Pacific Is.	European
Burt (NZ)	7.1 — 7.6	6.6 — 7.0	9.3 — 9.8	10.0 — 10.5	12.3 — 12.8*	12.3 — 12.8*
Schonell R1	7.5	7.5	9.5	9.9	11.6	12.1
Peters Spelling	6.6	7.6	9.9	9.8	12.7	12.3
Table 18	* Ceiling level of N.Z. norms on test.					

Finally Table 18 reports the lowest and highest scores of each subgroup. The ranges of scores were two to three years above and below the means.

7 Summary

Daily, individual instruction might be expected to produce important shifts in children's reading performance. The Reading Recovery programme was associated with such shifts in all the subgroups studied.

The challenges

Readers are asked to consider again the degree of challenge accepted by the Reading Recovery programme.

1   The children with the poorest performance of all the children in their schools at 6:0 were selected for instruction. Teachers used no procedures for excluding any children. They dealt with children in the tail of the achievement distribution for the age-group and included:

- bicultural Maori children
- bilingual Pacific Island children
- children with handicaps
- children awaiting Special Class placements

2   It was against normal expectations that any children in the tail end of the achievement distribution could be brought to average levels of attainment:

- in as little time as 13-14 weeks
- in both reading and writing.

Above-average levels of attainment would not be expected.

3 Whatever the level of attainment at the end of individual tutoring it would be against normal expectations for many children to retain average placements three years later given the ups and downs of school instruction and of child health and family circumstance.

4 It would be almost unreasonable to expect to get any shifts and maintenance of the kinds described with a partially implemented programme which means:

• children who entered school in Term III could not receive a full programme as it was only funded for the calendar year, and
• teachers in the field trial year were not operating the programme as prescribed.

Summary of gains to 1984

The Reading Recovery programme is an effective programme for reducing the number of children with reading difficulties in New Zealand schools (Clay, 1979; Clay and Watson, 1982). It is a second chance, early intervention programme. Its aim is to pick up the children who have not begun to read and write after one year at school and provide them with intensive instruction daily and individually. As a result of accelerated progress the children typically leave the programme with average levels of performance in three to six months. The success gained with the poorest performers of the age group at six years runs counter to the assumptions, expectations and experience in most Western education systems. It is probably related to the specific nature of the instruction delivered by well-trained teachers (Clay, 1982).

Since 1978 the programme has been developed and gradually expanded. Although it has only ever been partially implemented it has won support from teachers, principals, school committees, the Department of Education, the media and the public. Reports of its research and development phase, and of two follow-up studies (one and three years later) support its effectiveness across ethnic groups.

Quality assurance

The gains were achieved by experienced but nonspecialist primary teachers without academic training but who knew how to teach children of this age group, and how, in particular, to teach reading. They were guided by a few very well-trained tutors who fully understood why each of the procedures and requirements were in the programme. The Department of Education has ensured that the expansion of the programme only proceeds when this necessary support system is already in place. They have also ensured that clear communications to the rest of the education system preceded each expansion of the programme so that all understood the preventive thrust of the programme.

Training for teachers consists of only 50 hours distributed fortnightly throughout the year during the period that teachers are engaged in more than 400 hours of Reading Recovery teaching.

Training for tutors of teachers, who guide the Reading Recovery programme in their district, is a special, year-long University-based course which assumes that the tutor will also work as a Reading Recovery teacher.

Some recommendations

The follow-up studies point to some recommendations for Reading Recovery teachers, and their schools.

1 When children are to be included in a Reading Recovery programme contact parents and contract for regular attendance for this second chance learning opportunity. The school should co-operate with the family to establish appropriate home activities to follow-up on lessons.

2 Allow for sufficient time in the programme and apply discontinuing criteria conservatively especially with the Maori children.

3 Adopt a watch-dog role for ex-Reading Recovery children in the school and remind staff
• to monitor their progress sensitively,
• to consider their promotion carefully,
• to provide further individual help if needed and particularly if progress slows.
Although Reading Recovery children may perform well in their classes they remain at-risk children.

Readers with problems

Once this programme is fully implemented its impact within the education system will be felt as each age group moves up through the standard classes. There should be a drastic reduction in the numbers of children requiring special teaching for fundamental skills in reading and writing above the second year at school. Many more of the 'slow' children in schools should be able to perform close to average class levels in reading and writing and be able to use these achievements in the service of further learning. This programme will also contribute to the early identification, by 6½ years or eighteen months from school entry, of 'Third Wave' children requiring the attention of a reading specialist for a further year or two.

Gains for the education system

Some of the inefficiencies that have seemed unavoidable in the past should disappear. We should reduce the problems of the teacher in the upper primary or elementary school who tries to teach a nonreader but does not really know how to; the time spent by teachers with the 'low reading groups' should be reduced; the number of children on waiting lists for reading clinics should be reduced. Hopefully children needing continuing help should be able to move straight from Reading Recovery to a reading specialist and not have to wait for a place marking time in a classroom where the programme is beyond them.

Because the effects of the programme run counter to past experience it seems unwise to make undue claims for it. However, the three year follow-up research suggests that for those who get daily instruction in Reading Recovery the long-term effects were good for each of three ethnic groups, European, Maori and Pacific Island children.

The cost effectiveness of the programme depends upon how well it achieves its goal of average performance for most of the children. The programme addresses a problem of special education in that it provides for all children at the lower end of the achievement distribution at six years, without exception. It runs with a minimum of specialist staff. Most important, it is a special education programme which, if it works, reduces the need for specialist provision in the upper primary (or elementary) school and secondary school.

References and Further Reading

Aman, M. G. and Singh, N. M., Specific reading disorders: Concepts of etiology reconsidered. In K. D. Gadow and I. Bader, (Eds.) *Advances in Learning and Behavioural Disabilities,* Vol.2., Greenwich, Connecticut: JAI Press, 1983, 1-47.

Arvidson, G., *Alphabetical Spelling List.* Wellington: NZCER, 1960.

Clay, Marie M., 'Emergent Reading Behaviour'. Unpubl. doctoral dissertation, University of Auckland Library, 1966.

Clay, Marie M., *Observing Young Readers: Selected Papers.* Portsmouth, New Hampshire; Heinemann Educational Books, 1982.

Clay, Marie M., 'Reading errors and self-correction behaviour'. *British Journal of Educational Psychology,* 39, 1969. pp 47-56.

Clay, Marie M., Reading Recovery: A follow-up study. *New Zealand Journal of Educational Studies,* 15, 2, 1980. pp 137-155. (See also *Observing Young Readers.)*

Clay, Marie M., *Reading: The Patterning of Complex Behaviour.* Second Edition. Heinemann Educational Books, Auckland, 1979.

Clay, Marie M., 'Research on language and reading in Pakeha and Polynesian children', in D. K. Bracken and E. Malmquist (eds). *Improving Reading Ability Around The World,* International Reading Association, Newark, Delaware, 1970.

Clay, Marie M., 'The reading behaviour of five year old children: a research report'. *New Zealand Journal of Educational Studies,* 2(1), 1967, pp 11-31.

Clay, Marie M., The Reading Recovery project. In *The Early Detection of Reading Difficulties: A Diagnostic Survey and Reading Recovery Procedures.* Heinemann Publishers, Auckland, 1979.

Clay, Marie M., *What Did I Write?* Heinemann Educational Books, Auckland, 1975.

Clay, Marie M. and Watson, B., An inservice programme for Reading Recovery teachers. *Education,* 4, 1981, pp 22-27. (See also *Observing Young Readers.*)

Clay, Marie M. and Watson, B., 'The success of Maori children in the Reading Recovery programme'. Report to the Director of Research, Department of Education, Wellington, 1982.

Croft, C., *Spell-Write: An Aid to Writing, Spelling and Word Study.* Wellington: NZCER, 1983.

De Hirsch, Katrina; Jansky, J. and Longford, W. J., *Predicting the Failing Reader,* Harper and Row, New York, 1966.

Elkonin, D. B., USSR. In Downing, John. *Comparative Reading: Cross-National Studies of Behaviour and Processes in Reading and Writing.* Macmillan, New York, 1975.

Elley, W., Croft, C., and Cowie, C. *A New Zealand Basic Word List* Wellington: NZCER, 1977.

Fernald, Grace M., *Remedial Techniques in Basic School Subjects,* McGraw-Hill, New York, 1943.

Ferreiro, E. and Teberosky, A., *Literacy Before Schooling.* Portsmouth, New Hampshire; Heinemann Educational Books, 1982.

Genshi, C., Observational research methods for early childhood education. In B. Spodek, *Handbook of Research in Early Childhood Education,* New York: The Free Press, 1982.

Goodacre, Elizabeth, *Children and Learning to Read,* Routledge and Kegan Paul, London, 1971.

Goodman, K. S., 'Analysis of oral reading miscues: applied psycholinguistics', *Reading Research Quarterly,* 1, 1969, pp 9-30.

Goodman, Y. M. and Burke, C., *The Reading Miscue Inventory,* New York: Macmillan, 1972.

Guildford, J. P., *Fundamental Statistics in Psychology and Education,* Fourth Edition, McGraw-Hill, New York, 1965.

Hildreth, G., Early writing as an aid to reading. *Elementary English,* 40, 1964, pp 15-20.

Lyman, H. B., *Test Scores and What They Mean,* Prentice-Hall, Englewood Cliffs, New Jersey, 1963.

McLeod, J., *The Gap Reading Comprehension Test,* Heinemann Educational Books, Melbourne, 1965.

Neale, Marie D., *The Neale Analysis of Reading Ability,* Macmillan, London, 1958.

NZCER., *Progressive Achievement Tests of Reading Vocabulary and Reading Comprehension,* Wellington: NZCER, 1969.

Reid, Jessie, 'Learning to think about reading', *Educational Research,* 9,(1), 1966 pp 56-62.

Robinson, Susan M., Predicting Early Reading Progress, Unpubl. M.A. thesis, University of Auckland Library, 1973.

Smith, F., *Understanding Reading,* Second Edition. Holt Rhinehart and Winston, New York, 1978.

Strang, Ruth., *The Diagnostic Teaching of Reading,* McGraw-Hill, New York, 1969.

Wade, T., Promotion Patterns in the Junior School. Auckland: University of Auckland Library, Unpubl. Dip.Ed. Thesis, 1978.

Appendix

SUMMARY OF RUNNING RECORD

Name:_____ Date:_____ _____ D. of B._____ Age:___ yrs ___ mths

School:_____ Recorder:_____

SUMMARY OF RUNNING RECORD

Text Titles	Running Words Error	Error Rate	Accuracy	Self-Correction Rate
1. Easy _____	_____	1:_____	_____ %	1:_____
2. Instructional_____	_____	1:_____	_____ %	1:_____
3. Hard _____	_____	1:_____	_____ %	1:_____

Directional Movement _____

ANALYSIS OF ERRORS   Cues used and cues neglected

Easy _____

Instructional _____
_____

Hard _____
_____

CROSS CHECKING ON CUES

Page		E	SC	Cues Used* E SC

Page		E	SC	Cues Used*	
				E	SC

DIAGNOSTIC SUMMARY SHEET

Recommended for survey checks after one year of instruction

Name:_____ Date:_____ D. of B._____ Age:____yrs ____mths

School:_____

SUMMARY OF RUNNING RECORD

Text Titles	Running Words Error	Error Rate	Accuracy	Self-Correction Rate
1. Easy _____	_____	1:_____	_____%	1:_____
2. Instructional_____	_____	1:_____	_____%	1:_____
3. Hard _____	_____	1:_____	_____%	1:_____

Directional Movement _____

ANALYSIS OF ERRORS   Cues used and cues neglected

Easy _____

Instructional _____

_____

Hard _____

_____

Cross checking on cues

LETTER IDENTIFICATION

$\frac{}{54}$

CONCEPTS ABOUT PRINT   SAND   STONES

$\frac{}{24}$

WORD TEST (CLAY)   LIST A_____ LIST B_____ LIST C_____ $\frac{}{15}$

OTHER READING TEST (BURT-NZ, 1981) _____

WRITING SAMPLE	WRITING VOCABULARY	DICTATION	A B C D E	STORY	SPELLING
Language: Message: Direction:			$\frac{}{37}$		

Useful strategies on text:

Problem strategies on text:

Useful strategies with words:

Problem strategies with words:

Useful strategies with letters:

Problem strategies with letters:

SUMMARY:

SIGNATURE: _____

PROCESSING ANALYSIS SUMMARY SHEET : RECORD OF WORD SOLVING PROGRESS

NAME: _____

DATE: _____

ANALYSIS OF ERRORS

Text A or B or C	Count of Word Errors	Acceptable Graphic Cues								Syntax Acceptable	Semantics Acceptable
		Zero	Reversal	First	Last	Middle	First + Last	2 elements different	1 element different		

ANALYSIS OF WORD SOLVING

Silent/Audible Analysis							Self Correction				Count of Words Solved
Pause	1st Sound	1st Sounds	1st Syllable	Repetition	Syntax	Semantics	Sounds				
							First	Last	Middle		

Accuracy

Text A (Easy)   ____ / ____

Text B (Instructional)   ____ / ____

Text C (Hard)   ____ / ____

CALCULATION AND CONVERSION TABLES

Error Rate	Percent Accuracy
1 : 200	99.5
1 : 100	99
1 : 50	98
1 : 35	97
1 : 25	96
1 : 20	95
1 : 17	94
1 : 14	93
1 : 12.5	92
1 : 11.75	91
1 : 10	90
1 : 9	89
1 : 8	87.5
1 : 7	85.5
1 : 6	83
1 : 5	80
1 : 4	75
1 : 3	66
1 : 2	50

CALCULATIONS
RW = Running Words
E   = Errors
SC = Self-corrections

ERROR RATE

$$\frac{\text{Running words}}{\text{Errors}}$$

e.g. $\dfrac{150}{15}$ = Ratio 1 : 10

ACCURACY

$$100 - \frac{E}{RW} \times \frac{100}{1}$$

$$100 - \frac{15}{150} \times \frac{100}{1} \%$$

$$= 90\%$$

SELF-CORRECTION RATE

$$\frac{E + SC}{SC}$$

$$\frac{15 + 5}{5} = \text{Ratio 1 : 4}$$

CONCEPTS ABOUT PRINT SCORE SHEET

Date:_____

Name:_____ Age:_____ TEST SCORE: | /24 |

Recorder:_____ Date of Birth:_____

STANINE GROUP: | |

PAGE	SCORE	ITEM	COMMENT
Cover		1. Front of book	
2/3		2. Print contains message	
4/5		3. Where to start	
4/5		4. Which way to go	
4/5		5. Return sweep to left	
4/5		6. Word by word matching	
6		7. First and last concept	
7		8. Bottom of picture	
8/9		9. Begin 'The' (Sand) or 'I' (Stones) bottom line, top OR turn book	
10/11		10. Line order altered	
12/13		11. Left page before right	
12/13		12. One change in word order	
12/13		13. One change in letter order	
14/15		14. One change in letter order	
14/15		15. Meaning of ?	
16/17		16. Meaning of full stop	
16/17		17. Meaning of comma	
16/17		18. Meaning of quotation marks	
16/17		19. Locate M m H h (Sand) OR T t B b (Stones)	
18/19		20. Reversible words was, no	
20		21. One letter: two letters	
20		22. One word: two words	
20		23. First and last letter of word	
20		24. Capital letter	

LETTER IDENTIFICATION SCORE SHEET

Date:_____

Name:_____ Age:_____

TEST SCORE: | /54

Recorder:_____ Date of Birth:_____

STANINE GROUP: |

	A	S	Word	I.R.		A	S	Word	I.R.
A					a				
F					f				
K					k				
P					p				
W					w				
Z					z				
B					b				
H					h				
O					o				
J					j				
U					u				
					a				
C					c				
Y					y				
L					l				
Q					q				
M					m				
D					d				
N					n				
S					s				
X					x				
I					i				
E					e				
G					g				
R					r				
V					v				
T					t				
					g				

Confusions:

Letters Unknown:

Comment:

Recording:

A Alphabet response: tick (check)

S Letter sound response: tick (check)

Word Record the word the child gives

IR Incorrect response: Record what the child says

TOTALS

TOTAL SCORE |

WORD TEST SCORE SHEET

Use any **one** list of words.

Date:_____

TEST SCORE: [ ] /15

Name:_____ Age:_____

Recorder:_____ Date of Birth:_____

STANINE GROUP: [ ]

Record incorrect responses beside word

LIST A	LIST B	LIST C
I	and	Father
Mother	to	come
are	will	for
here	look	a
me	he	you
shouted	up	at
am	like	school
with	in	went
car	where	get
children	Mr	we
help	going	they
not	big	ready
too	go	this
meet	let	boys
away	on	please

COMMENT:

WRITING VOCABULARY TEST SHEET

Name:_____ Age:_____ Date:_____

TEST SCORE: [   ]

Recorder:_____ Date of Birth:_____ STANINE GROUP: [   ]

(Fold heading under before child uses sheet)

- -

COMMENT

DICTATION TEST SHEET

Name:_____ Age:_____ Date:_____

TEST SCORE: | /37

Recorder:_____ Date of Birth:_____

STANINE GROUP:

(Fold heading under before child uses sheet)

- -

COMMENT

NAME:

LESSON PLAN

NEW TEXT	RE-READING	STRATEGIES 1 USED 2 PROMPTED	WORD ANALYSIS	1 LETTER IDENTIFICATION 2 LETTER FORMATION

READING

TASK	WORD ANALYSIS AND FLUENCY PRACTICE	SPATIAL CONCEPTS	SEQUENCING	COMMENT

WRITING

CUT UP STORY

WEEKLY RECORD OF WRITING VOCABULARY

Name: _____

Date of Birth: _____

Initial Testing Date:	Week: Date:	Week: Date:	Week: Date:	Week: Date:	Week: Date:
Week: Date:	Week: Date:	Week: Date:	Week: Date:	Week: Date:	

RECOMMENDATIONS FOR DISCONTINUING CHILDREN

Name:_____

Date:_____

School:_____

1 SETTING (Same class, new class, book level, teacher's reaction, size of group etc.)

2 SURVIVAL (Detail what behaviours will ensure coping in group instruction)

3 RUNNING RECORD ANALYSIS (Detail cues used and cues neglected)

4 COMMENT ON IMPROVEMENTS SINCE PREVIOUS SUMMARY AND PREDICTIONS

RECOMMENDATIONS: (for class teacher, or further teaching or further assessment)

Signed:_____

SUMMARY TESTING AND RECOMMENDATIONS

Name:_____

Date of Birth:_____

School:_____

SUMMARY OF RUNNING RECORD

Text Titles	Running Words Error	Error Rate	Accuracy	Self-Correction Rate

Initial Test   Date:_____

1. Easy _____ _____ 1:_____ _____% 1:_____
2. Instructional _____ _____ 1:_____ _____% 1:_____
3. Hard _____ _____ 1:_____ _____% 1:_____

Retest   Date:_____

1. Easy _____ _____ 1:_____ _____% 1:_____
2. Instructional _____ _____ 1:_____ _____% 1:_____
3. Hard _____ _____ 1:_____ _____% 1:_____

_____ Date:_____

1. Easy _____ _____ 1:_____ _____% 1:_____
2. Instructional _____ _____ 1:_____ _____% 1:_____
3. Hard _____ _____ 1:_____ _____% 1:_____

TESTS	L.I. 54	Stanine	C.A.P. 24	Stanine	Word Test 15	Stanine	Reading Test Score	Writing	Stanine	Dictation 37	Stanine
Initial test Date:											
Retest Date:											

RECOMMENDATIONS: (for class teacher, or for review, or further teaching, or further assessment)

Stanine Score Summary Sheet

'Ready to Read' Word Test

320 urban children	Stanine Score	1	2	3	4	5	6	7	8	9
aged 5:0 — 7:0 in 1968	Test Score	0	0	1	2-5	6-12	13-14	—	15	—

282 urban children	Stanine Score	1	2	3	4	5	6	7	8	9
aged 6:0 — 7:3 in 1978	Test Score	0-1	2-5	6-9	10-12	13-14	—	15	—	—

Letter Identification

320 urban children	Stanine Score	1	2	3	4	5	6	7	8	9
aged 5:0 — 7:0 in 1968	Test Score	—	0	2-7	8-25	26-47	48-52	53	54	—

282 urban children	Stanine Score	1	2	3	4	5	6	7	8	9
aged 6:0 — 7:3 in 1978	Test Score	0-13	14-28	29-43	44-49	50-52	53	—	54	—

Concepts About Print

320 urban children	Stanine Score	1	2	3	4	5	6	7	8	9
aged 5:0 — 7:0 in 1968	Test Score	0	1-4	5-7	8-11	12-14	15-17	18-20	21-22	23-24

282 urban children	Stanine Score	1	2	3	4	5	6	7	8	9
aged 6:0 — 7:3 in 1978	Test Score	0-9	10-11	12-13	14-16	17-18	19	20-21	22	23-24

Writing Vocabulary

282 urban children	Stanine Score	1	2	3	4	5	6	7	8	9
aged 6:0 — 7:3 in 1978	Test Score	0-13	14-19	20-28	29-35	36-45	46-55	56-70	71-80	81-

Dictation

282 urban children	Stanine Score	1	2	3	4	5	6	7	8	9
aged 6:0 — 7:3 in 1978	Test Score	0-3	4-9	10-17	18-27	28-31	32-35	36-37	—	—

Index